MEDICAL LIABILITY

IN A NUTSHELL

SECOND EDITION

By

MARCIA MOBILIA BOUMIL
Assistant Professor of Family
Medicine and Community Health
Tufts University School of Medicine

CLIFFORD E. ELIAS
Professor of Law
Suffolk University Law School

DIANE BISSONETTE MOES
Donoghue, Barrett, & Singal
Boston, MA

THOMSON
™
WEST

Mat #40076620

Nutshell Series, In a Nutshell, the Nutshell Logo and West Group are trademarks registered in the U.S. Patent and Trademark Office.

COPYRIGHT © 1995 WEST PUBLISHING CO.
COPYRIGHT © 2003 By West, a Thomson business
          610 Opperman Drive
          P.O. Box 64526
          St. Paul, MN 55164–0526
          1–800–328–9352

ISBN 0–314–14295–9

*TEXT IS PRINTED ON 10% POST
CONSUMER RECYCLED PAPER*

∞

PREFACE

When the first edition of this text was published in 1995, we observed that the need for a new book on medical liability appeared to arise approximately every ten years. The first Nutshell book on medical malpractice was written in 1977 by Professor Joseph H. King Jr. He expressed the view that the law of medical malpractice was, for many years, an esoteric field into which few ventured with confidence. He also expressed the hope that his book would remove some of the mystery. That first edition fulfilled his wish and presented a sense of order to a then complex field.

The second edition to Professor King's book was published in 1986. It continued the effort to bring understanding and symmetry to the trends, which were developing, such as the broadened theory of informed consent.

Then, almost ten years later, in 1995, it was apparent that another edition would not suffice. It has become necessary to write a new text in a field that had attracted enormous attention from the Congress, state legislatures, physicians and trial lawyers. The field had become identified clearly enough to warrant the inclusion of a variety of medical liability courses in the curricula of many law schools.

The time span between the publication of texts on medical liability has again shortened. Eight years later, the need for a substantially new text was recognized. This Nutshell is not intended to cover every aspect of the field of medical liability. However, we found it necessary to add two new chapters, "Medical Technology," and "Liability of Managed Care Organizations." We have given more attention to other topics, such as telemedicine. The authors express the hope that law students and members of the legal profession will benefit form it. It has been written, as well, for health care professionals, such as physicians, legislators and administrators of hospitals and other health care organizations.

We are indebted to a number of individuals for their involvement in our endeavor. Suffolk University law students, in particular, provided us with research and writing assistance. Our deepest appreciation is extended to Magdalena Parnell, Sandra Desjardins, Kelly Holody, Sheila Bonafonti, Richard Zabbo, Lynn Zuchowski, Robert Kirsh, and Jonathan Glazier, law students who worked diligently for a period of almost two years, providing us not only with invaluable assistance, but also with guidance. Professor Elias's secretary at Suffolk Law School, Mara Felt, provider her usual high-quality skills, willingly and cheerfully.

MARCIA MOBILIA BOUMIL
CLIFFORD E. ELIAS
DIANE BISSONNETTE MOES

Boston, Massachusetts

OUTLINE

OUTLINE

*

TABLE OF CASES

References are to Pages

TABLE OF CASES

*

TABLE OF STATUTES

UNITED STATES

UNITED STATES CODE ANNOTATED
29 U.S.C.A.—Labor

42 U.S.C.A.—The Public Health and Welfare

TABLE OF STATUTES

TABLE OF STATUTES

TABLE OF STATUTES

NEW YORK, MCKINNEY'S PUBLIC HEALTH LAW

OHIO REVISED CODE

VERNON'S ANNOTATED TEXAS CIVIL STATUTES

FEDERAL RULES OF CIVIL PROCEDURE

FEDERAL RULES OF EVIDENCE

UNIFORM CONTRIBUTION AMONG TORTFEASORS ACT

CODE OF FEDERAL REGULATIONS

MEDICAL LIABILITY

IN A NUTSHELL

SECOND EDITION

*

CHAPTER ONE

ESTABLISHING THE PROFESSIONAL RELATIONSHIP

I. IN GENERAL: NEGLIGENCE THEORY

Since much of medical malpractice litigation relies upon negligence theory, it is important to clearly establish the elements of the negligence cause of action. Negligence is defined as conduct that falls below the standard established by law for protection against unreasonable risk of harm. There are four major elements required for a negligence action: (1) that an actor owes a duty of care to another; (2) that the applicable standard for carrying out the duty be breached; (3) that as a proximate cause of the breach of duty a compensable injury results; and (4) that there be compensable damages or injury to the plaintiff.

II. DUTY

In medical malpractice litigation the existence of a "duty" generally refers to an obligation of the defendant (whether it be an organization, physician or other health professional) to another individual

1

(who is generally, but not always, a patient). The duty may refer to the physician's obligation to act or refrain from acting in a particular way; it may refer to the information that he communicates to his patient prior to acting; or it may refer to any of numerous obligations that a physician incurs upon entering into a professional relationship. It does, however, require that there be such a relationship, express or implied, before the applicable duty of care is owed. Thus a physician who declines to render care, and who has otherwise not undertaken to do so (for example, by previously agreeing to accept certain patients) is generally under no obligation and incurs no liability for failing to enter into a professional relationship.

Traditionally, at common law, there was a distinction between misfeasance (active wrongdoing) and nonfeasance (mere inaction). Misfeasance could be the subject of liability since the actor undertook an obligation and thereafter carried it out in a negligent manner, whereas nonfeasance would not subject the actor to liability because neither he undertook nor the law imposed upon him any duty to act or avoid injury. There are now many exceptions to the common law. Nevertheless, the existence of a duty is still critical to any negligence action, and failure to establish that element is generally fatal to a cause of action.

The duty of the medical practitioner is generally defined by the nature of the professional relationship. A specialist in one area may incur a duty to treat certain related conditions, but may have no duty to undertake treatment of other unrelated conditions, even if they are urgent or life-threatening. Similarly, an emergency room physician may have an obligation to treat anyone who presents himself for treatment in that setting, but on his way home incurs no liability for failing to stop and treat a passerby. In a free society individuals are not forced to undertake obligations that they decline to accept, as long as there is no implication of acceptance on the basis of an affirmative action. Like all other marketable services, the delivery of medical services is a voluntary undertaking with no requirement, absent a specific intent, to accept the obligation.

Although the existence of a physician-patient relationship is the hallmark of finding a duty of care, courts may, at times, be quick to find that a duty does, in fact, exist on the basis of the circumstances. As a result, most physicians will not decline to provide necessary services, particularly under emergency circumstances, so that some form of medical care is generally available to those who seek it. Even hospitals that, historically, could choose the patients they would admit and the circumstances of admission are constrained by numerous factors that today limit their discretion.

As hospitals determine their own admission criteria, they need to be sensitive to numerous potential constraints which may limit their ability to select patients according to preference. For example, those hospitals that receive any significant form of public assistance are forbidden from discriminating against patients on the basis of race, national origin or handicap. Those hospitals that received construction funds under the federally-sponsored Hill–Burton Act had an obligation to provide some level of uncompensated care to those unable to pay. (Virtually all Hill–Burton obligations have now been fulfilled.) In addition, certain statutory or constitutional provisions, as well as an institution's own charter, may affect admission practices, particularly for public hospitals. In the event that a court finds that a patient was wrongfully denied services, the court will imply a duty of care, and hold the facility liable for whatever injury was proximately caused by the failure to act. See Chapter 8.

A. EMERGENCY CIRCUMSTANCES

This is not to say that most hospitals, particularly private entities, are not free to determine their own admission policies as long as they are not discriminatory. The major exception to this general principle pertains to emergency facilities and hospitals offering emergency care. As to those facilities, the general rule is that emergency treatment must be provided to anyone presenting an emergent situation. See 42 U.S.C.A. § 1395dd (EMTALA) In some states this is also required by local statute; in others it is imposed by licensing requirements or health regulations. Furthermore, the developing case law imposes a duty on emergency facilities to provide such services and make them available to anyone who presents himself in an emergency situation.

There are two reasons for the imposition of such a duty. First, it is consistent with public health principles and codes for individuals requiring emergency services to be able to access the nearest emergency facility without jeopardizing their condition in seeking a more remote facility. Secondly, by indicating to the public that a certain facility offers emergency care, an individual in need of services will rely on being treated there and not lose valuable time going to such a facility, only to be turned away.

On the other hand, if a patient arrives in an emergent condition which a particular facility is utterly unable to handle because of the type of problem and the medical personnel available, the only liability that will likely arise (barring actual negligence in staffing) comes from the duty to exercise due care in identifying the situation and preparing the patient for transfer to an appropriate facility. Courts are increasingly likely to impose a duty of care and hold an emergency facility liable for withholding treatment that could have been rendered if it results in further harm to the patient.

A hospital or other facility which provides emergency services to a patient who might otherwise be refused services does not necessary obligate itself to render further services once the patient is stabilized and the emergency passes. Thus the duty imposed by the emergent condition extends only so long as that condition exists. Once a patient is stabilized, an ongoing physician-patient relationship is not necessarily established which might require the physician or facility to provide follow up or other care. The implied duty that is imposed by the emergency is thus different than the obligation that arises in the context of a consensual physician-patient relationship. See Chapter 8.

B.   CONSENSUAL RELATIONSHIPS

A duty of care from physician to patient generally arises in the context of voluntary or consensual physician-patient relationship. An express (if not stated) agreement is entered when the physician agrees to provide treatment consistent with his abilities (generalist or specialist) and the patient's desire. The treatment is expected to meet a certain standard of care. The patient agrees to pay or arrange payment for the services (unless the physician agrees otherwise) and to generally cooperate with the treatment plan. It is important to note that even if the payment is reduced or the services are rendered free of charge, the same duty of care applies, as long as the physician-patient relationship is consensual as to both parties. Furthermore, even if there was not an express offer and acceptance for services to be rendered, courts may still imply that such a relationship existed if the totality of the circumstances so indicate.

What if a physician agrees to treat a patient but, after evaluation, changes his mind? The existence of a physician-patient relationship and the obligations that arise therefrom may depend upon the circumstances of the case. If, for example, an appointment is made some time in advance, and the patient presents the physician with a condition that is time sensitive (e.g., diabetes, which requires regular and periodic treatment), the physician is likely to be obligated to provide treatment or make an immediate and appropriate referral so that the patient's condition is not jeopardized in waiting for another physician.

Suppose, instead, that an examination is made and the physician determines that the necessary treatment is not within his capability or expertise? Referral to another physician is proper, and the initial practitioner should make sure that a suitable and timely referral is made. It is not appropriate, for example, to direct the patient to the American Medical Association for a referral; it is also not adequate to refer a patient to another practitioner who is unable or unwilling to treat the patient. On the other hand, a patient cannot refuse an appropriate referral, and thereafter insist that the referring physician continue to treat him on the basis of an ongoing duty.

Sometimes patients are brought to physicians in a condition that renders a voluntary or consensual relationship impractical. The patient may be unconscious, incompetent or otherwise incapable of manifesting an intent to enter a physician-patient relationship. In those cases the court may nevertheless be justified in finding the existence of a relationship, despite the lack of mutuality of assent. Indeed, the court may find that another person acting on behalf of the unconscious or incompetent patient entered into a physician-patient relationship. Such a relationship can either be implied-in-fact or implied-in-law. If, for example, a relative brings the patient in for treatment and expressly assents to services, a contract is said to be implied in fact. If, on the other hand, a patient is brought into an emergency room by police or rescue workers and in need of emergency services, assent to treatment is said to be implied in law. The patient, as a beneficiary of the "contract" between the person acting on his behalf and the physician, takes on the same rights and obligations as though as an express contract had been made. Moreover, both the physician and the beneficiary are entitled to enforce its terms.

Merely because a physician is consulted regarding a patient does not, however, subject the physician to the duties of a physician-patient relationship. A number of cases have addressed the issues of contacts made over the telephone. Whether or not a professional relationship results from such a contact depends upon the facts of the case. For example, if a patient telephones a physician in an effort to secure a diagnosis or treatment, and the physician undertakes to render such service, the court could conclude that a physician-patient relationship was established. See *O'Neill v. Montefiore Hospital* (N.Y.A.D.1960) (A physician who spoke to a patient over the telephone from an emergency room could have been found to undertake a physician-patient relationship). On the other hand, it is not a necessary result that merely consulting over the telephone obligates the physician to a duty of care. Moreover, if a physician informally consults a colleague about a patient's condition, whether or not the patient is identified, the informal opinion is unlikely to result in a finding that a physician-patient relationship exists. See *Oliver v. Brock* (Ala. 1976) (Informal consult in which primary physician recorded his conversation with a colleague in the patient's medical record did not give rise to a physician-patient relationship between patient and colleague). Note, however, that a conversation between a treating physician and a colleague that he consults may give rise to a physician-patient relationship between the consulting physician and the patient. See *Lection v. Dyll* (Tex. App.2001) (On-call neurologist who, during telephone consultation with emergency room physician, diagnosed patient's condition and indicated treatment could have been found to undertake a physician-patient relationship). These cases must be distinguished, of course, from those involving an actual or requested consultation or second opinion in which the consulting physician does establish a traditional physician-patient relationship.

Yet another situation was presented in *Giallanza v. Sands* (Fla.App.1975) where it appeared that a physician allowed his name to be used for the purpose of having a patient admitted to a hospital. The physician testified that he informed the staff that he would not be treating the patient; in fact, he had no contact whatsoever with the patient or her family. The court held that it was a triable issue of fact as to whether a physician-patient relationship had been created.

Notwithstanding the seeming willingness of courts to impose a duty of care arising out of a physician-patient relationship, there are some circumstances where courts draw the line. For example, in *Rainer v. Grossman* (Cal.App.1973), a medical school professor was sued by a patient who claimed that the professor had offered an opinion about a course of treatment after hearing about the patient's history. The appellate court upheld the trial court's dismissal of the action against the professor, stating that no physician-patient relationship could be established since the professor had no opportunity to control the actions of the treating physician. Furthermore, to hold otherwise would violate principles of academic freedom in which faculty members are encouraged to disseminate knowledge for the benefit of all.

C.   DUTY TO NON–PATIENTS

While the presence of a physician-patient relationship is necessary to establish a duty on the part of the physician, it does not necessarily follow that once the relationship is found, it extends only to the patient. An obvious example is the physician who treats a pregnant woman and consequently incurs a duty of care to both mother and unborn child. In *Sylvia v. Gobeille* (R.I.1966), a physician neglected to prescribe gamma globulin for a pregnant woman after he knew she was exposed to German measles. As a result, her child was born with serious birth defects. The court held that a cause of action could be maintained by the child—a third party. In such a case, the plaintiff could probably plead a cause of action grounded upon both a third party beneficiary theory and an undertaking theory in tort based upon the treatment of the mother.

Duties to third parties, however, extend beyond the immediate duty to a third-party beneficiary. In *Shepard v. Redford Community Hospital* (Mich.App. 1986), a woman sought emergency care complaining of high fever, leg pain, congestion, headaches and weakness. She was diagnosed with a respiratory infection and discharged. Two days later, her son suffered from the same symptoms, and was hospitalized immediately. He died that same day after being diagnosed with spinal meningitis. In the wrongful death action that followed, the mother claimed that her misdiagnosis and improper treatment resulted in the death of her son. The claim was dismissed by the trial court on the basis that there was no physician-patient relationship between the doctor and the son, and thus no duty. However, the appellate court reversed, holding that the relationship between mother and physician gave rise to a "special relationship" which could result in a duty of care on behalf of the son.

Similarly, in *Bradshaw v. Daniel* (Tenn.1993), a patient was admitted to the emergency room with symptoms of the disease, Rocky Mountain Spotted Fever, and ultimately died of that illness only a day later. Although the physician communicated with the patient's wife, he never warned her that because of the circumstances under which the patient contracted the disease, she might also be at risk. The disease was not communicable, but both may have exposed to it at the same time. When she later came down with similar symptoms, and thereafter died of the illness, a suit was brought on her behalf alleging that the physician failed to warn her that she, too, might be at risk. The trial court dismissed the claim on the basis that there was no duty to warn a non-patient of the risk of exposure to a non-communicable disease. The Supreme Court of Tennessee reversed, however, concluding that the existence of the physician-patient relationship with the husband was adequate to impose an affirmative duty of care to warn persons in his immediate family about the risks concerning that illness.

There is also a line of cases beginning with *Tarasoff v. Regents of the University of California* (Cal. 1976), in which courts have considered the duty of a psychiatrist to third persons who might be injured by dangerous patients. In *Tarasoff*, the court found that a psychiatrist affiliated with the defendant should have known that his patient was dangerous and that an identifiable victim was the subject of his violent aggression. The court held that the physician had a duty to take reasonable steps to protect third parties, assuming the psychiatrist knew or should have known that his patient posed a risk of serious bodily harm and a specific target could be identified. Numerous other cases have since followed suit (See, e.g., *Bardoni v. Kim* (Mich.App. 1986)), although not all jurisdictions are uniform in their approach to these cases, nor do they all reach a similar result.

Not all situations in which the obligations of a provider affect third persons (not a party to the physician-patient relationship) result in liability of the provider. For example, in *Chatman v. Millis* (Ark.1975), a divorced woman sought the services of a psychologist to determine whether her son's father might be sexually abusing him. After examining the child, the psychologist concluded that there was a likelihood of such abuse, and provided a report to that effect that was subsequently used in court. The psychologist, who was thereafter sued by the boy's father for an allegedly negligent diagnosis, defended on the basis that he had no physician-patient relationship with the father. The court agreed that no duty, and therefore no cause of action, existed on behalf of the father who was neither a patient nor a beneficiary of the professional who provided services.

One area that has seen voluminous litigation involving the rights of third parties is the employment context. Typically the issue is whether a physician who is engaged by an employer to perform an examination of an employee incurs a duty to the examinee to perform non-negligently. Usually one of two circumstances result from an allegedly negligent examination: either the patient is denied initial or continued employment, or the physician fails to discover a significant condition that might have been treated had it been diagnosed. Related cases have occurred in other contexts, such as when a physician employed by a life insurance company negligently examines an applicant, and insurance coverage is denied as a result. Courts have not been uniform in their holdings.

The case of *Green v. Walker* (5th Cir.1990) is an example of the employment context. The plaintiff's employer required him to submit to an annual physical examination as a condition of employment. The defendant physician engaged to perform the exam reported that all tests were normal and gave the highest possible rating. When another physician examined the plaintiff a year later, he was diagnosed with lung cancer. The patient sued the employer's physician claiming that the physician failed to discover his condition. The defendant's motion for summary judgment was granted on the basis that the physician, who was engaged by the employer, had no physician-patient relationship with the plaintiff and thus owed no duty of care to him. The federal court of appeals, sitting in a diversity case, reversed, holding that where an employee is required as a condition of employment to submit to examination, a physician-patient relationship is established. The court held that this relationship results in an obligation of due care, at least to the extent of the examination. This duty includes the obligation to make a reasonable and timely effort to communicate to the examinee any findings that pose an imminent threat to his or her well-being.

The requirement that the claimant be examined does not necessarily establish a physician-patient relationship with an adverse party's agent, however, and no express or implied duty necessarily arises. In *Keene v. Wiggins* (Cal.App.1977) an employee received worker's compensation benefits as a result of an injury sustained on the job. The employer engaged the defendant physician to review the matter, indicating his prognosis, including permanent disability. The physician diagnosed the plaintiff's condition as not amenable to further treatment, which diagnosis the plaintiff claimed that he relied upon. In a lawsuit that followed, the physician defended on the basis that no physician-patient relationship existed, and thus any duty extended only to the employer. The court agreed that in the absence of any special circumstances, it would be unusual for a claimant to rely on the report of a physician engaged by an adverse party.

A contrary result holding that a duty of care did exist in similar circumstances was reached in *Webb v. T.D.* (Mont.1997). In that case, a physician who performed an independent examination of a worker at the request of her employer's workers' compensation carrier was held to owe a duty of care to the worker. This duty included the physician exercising ordinary care to discover and communicate conditions posing imminent danger to the worker's physical or mental well-being.

III. THE LIMITS OF DUTY

Like most other agreements, those between physician and patient that result in the delivery of medical care can also be ended. Often they end in due course when the treatment is completed or when the patient dies or moves away from the area. Sometimes the physician-patient relationship ends when either the patient or both parties agree that another physician will take over treatment of the patient. Sometimes the professional relationship ends because the physician determines that he no longer wants to treat the patient. This can occur for a number of reasons, including failure to pay for services, failure to show up for appointments, refusal to follow the treatment plan, and the physician's change of practice. The general rule is that a physician is entitled to terminate the professional relationship only after he has given the patient reasonable notice and opportunity to secure the services of another competent physician. The reasonableness of the opportunity to make alternate provisions depends upon the length of time given, the willingness of the physician to assist in locating a new practitioner, and the information provided to the patient informing him about the status of his medical needs and future course of treatment.

A. VOLUNTARY TERMINATION

In the event that a patient requires emergent care before actual termination, or an acute problem requires treatment before a referral is completed, the attending physician will likely owe a duty of continuing care until the condition stabilizes. Furthermore, a practitioner who terminates a patient and makes a referral might still be held liable for foreseeable complications if the referral is not made to a suitable practitioner. In *Longman v. Jasiek* (Ill.App.1980), for example, a dentist specializing in oral surgery operated on a patient prior to terminating her as a patient. When she thereafter developed complications, the dentist referred her to her family physician. The family physician was not successful in treating a post-operative infection, and the patient sued the dentist for failing to provide post-operative care or make a suitable referral to an oral surgeon. The dentist was ultimately held liable for the post-operative complications which likely would have been avoided if a proper referral was completed. Thus *Longman* demonstrates that merely making a referral may not be adequate to defend against a charge of abandonment; the subsequent practitioner must also be suitable to meet the patient's needs. Furthermore, the referring physician may be liable not only for failing to inform the patient that a particular type of specialist is desirable, but also for a delay in obtaining subsequent care if a proper referral is not secured immediately.

The question of whether there are some circumstances in which a physician is precluded from terminating care of a patient is a difficult one. Under most circumstances, a physician who makes a proper referral offering suitable time and guidance is likely to avoid a later claim that he abandoned his patient. But what about a physician who expressly or implicitly agrees to render a particular course of treatment and wants to terminate the relationship before the services are completed? And what about a physician who agrees to perform a certain procedure but thereafter changes his mind and cannot find a subsequent practitioner? If a court ultimately finds that a contract was breached, an action may lie for damages consequent to the breach. This might include the time and expenses of pre-operative care (diagnostic tests, lab and x-ray costs, etc.) as well as any injury or deterioration in condition that the patient suffered as a result of the breach.

Causes of action for improper termination generally allege the tort of abandonment. A patient may be said to be abandoned when a physician interrupts a course of necessary treatment without proper notice and referral to a subsequent practitioner. This is sometimes referred to as an intentional abandonment. It should be distinguished from a negligent abandonment, which may be alleged when a physician, in the course of treatment, fails to attend to a patient as would reasonably be required under the circumstances. If, for example, a patient is prematurely discharged (see, e.g., *Wickline v. State* (Cal.App.1986)), this may give rise to a negligence action for abandonment and will be discussed further in Chapter 2, infra. Setting aside the confusion in terminology, the practical distinction is an evidentiary one: negligence actions generally require expert testimony as to the reasonable standard of care whereas intentional torts may be established on the basis of the deliberateness of the defendant's conduct.

In some situations, interruptions in the physician-patient relationship occur under circumstances that may be thought to excuse any neglect or conscious abandonment of the patient. For example, if the physician becomes ill or incapacitated himself, he may be temporarily or permanently unable to treat his patients. He also may or may not be able to provide reasonable notice or arrange alternative care. Generally, no liability results when a physician terminates treatment due to his own incapacity.

Another circumstance arises when physicians are unavailable when called upon due to prior emergencies, vacations, professional engagements or merely because they are not "on-call" when the need for their services exists. The law recognizes that medical necessities occur around the clock and no physician is expected to be available whenever the need arises. The obligation is to provide "reasonable" substitute care and to make patients aware of the exigencies that may require their care to be handled by another practitioner. For example, a rotation schedule of on-call physicians is a common practice to cover emergency patients or others who routinely require services at unpredictable times (e.g., expectant mothers). Except in those cases in which a physician specifically agrees to attend to a particular medical procedure, the use of substitute or on-call physicians is generally acceptable. Even then, if the physician is unavailable due to a prior emergency, abandonment should not occur. Of course, under such circumstances it is appropriate and necessary for the physician to explain the possible contingencies that might require another physician to attend to the patient.

Under circumstances where it is usual and customary for physicians to call upon their colleagues to substitute for them, the customary practice is to notify patients of the on-call system as well as the identity of those physicians who participate. Some courts hold that specific notice need not be given to patients as long as the substitute physician is competent. See *Beatty v. Morgan* (Ga.App.1984). This is a minority view, however, and most courts adhere to the customary practice.

The need to select competent physicians to rotate on an on-call basis should be underscored. The general rule is that another physician is not liable for the professional misconduct of a physician who covers his practice (See *Settoon v. St. Paul Fire & Marine Ins. Co.* (La.App.1976)) (declining to hold one physician vicariously liable for the malpractice of another on-call physician). However, he may incur direct liability if he fails to select competent physicians with whom to share an on-call rotation. See infra, chapter 7. By the same token, a physician who relies upon others to substitute for him may also incur liability if he neglects to provide adequate instructions or flag the special needs of a patient. See *Reams v. Stutler* (Ky.1982).

Intentional abandonment of a patient can either be express or implied. In those cases in which a physician notifies his patients that he no longer intends to provide services but fails to provide a suitable alternative, or even allow enough time for the patient to do so, the abandonment is said to be express. See *Norton v. Hamilton* (Ga.App.1955) (physician withdrew from treatment of pregnant woman; patient delivered before she was allegedly able to find another physician). Abandonment is said to be implied if the physician acts in such a way as to deny treatment without expressly terminating the professional relationship. For example, if a patient appears for emergency care and a physician turns the patient away claiming that no treatment is needed, this might constitute an implied abandonment. Alternatively, if a physician refuses to provide a proper referral (including medical history) so that another physician can take over a patient's treatment, this may constitute an implied abandonment. See *Johnson v. Vaughn* (Ky.1963) (patient of one physician called upon another physician for emergency treatment; second physician called initial physician for release, but was not able to secure the necessary information in a suitable and timely fashion).

B.   REFUSAL TO PROVIDE TREATMENT

The question of whether a single physician, facility or group practice can decline to treat certain patients is a difficult one. In *Payton v. Weaver* (Cal.App.1982), a physician attempted to terminate his care of an end-stage renal patient who required kidney dialysis in order to maintain her life. The patient was reported to be intensely uncooperative, frequently missed or was late for appointments and refused to follow the physician's instructions for treatment, including obtaining treatment for her drug and alcohol dependency. The physician provided reasonable notice of termination, but the patient was unable to secure alternative treatment and thus petitioned the court for an order compelling further treatment. The parties entered a stipulation regarding treatment, which was subsequently violated by the patient. When the physician petitioned the court again for an order permitting termination, the court granted his request, even though no other dialysis unit was willing to take on the patient's care. The order of the trial court was affirmed on appeal, at least in part because there was evidence that the patient's participation in the program adversely affected other patients.

A contrary result, however, was reached in another California decision. In *Leach v. Drummond Medical Group, Inc.* (Cal.App.1983), the plaintiffs were patients of a particular medical group. Dissatisfied with the performance of some of the physicians, the plaintiffs wrote to the state licensing board alleging a variety of complaints. When the group was notified of the allegations, it notified the plaintiffs of its intent to terminate their relationship on the basis that "a proper physician-patient relationship" could no longer be maintained. The plaintiffs sued, alleging a variety of causes of action, including one under the state civil rights act. After initially being denied relief by the trial court, the appellate court reversed. Finding that the complaint did state a claim upon which relief could be granted, the court held that while one physician may decline to treat a patient, an entire group (or hospital) did not necessarily have the same option. In that particular case, the group provided the only similar services available within approximately one hundred miles.

Finally, there are some circumstances under which a physician may have an ongoing obligation to former patients even after the termination of the physician-patient relationship. In a number of the *Dalkon Shield* cases, for example, physicians implanted the Dalkon Shield intrauterine device (IUD) in some patients with whom they later lost contact. When it became generally known within the profession that the Dalkon Shield had been linked to severe health risks, including sterility and even death, a number of courts held that the physicians incurred a duty to warn users of the potential hazards. A number of cases were brought upon physicians' failure to do so, some of which were successful. See *Tresemer v. Barke* (Cal.App.1978). Physicians, being in the best position to warn such patients, were generally obligated to make reasonable efforts to locate former patients and remove the device, if warranted.

Notwithstanding some of the foregoing exceptions, physicians are generally not obligated to treat patients whom they simply do not like. If a physician-patient relationship has already been initiated, proper notice of termination is necessary, along with those measures reasonably necessary to secure treatment with another physician. The law does not require that a subsequent treating physician be in place. *Payton* demonstrates that termination can occur even if no other physician can be found to assume the patient's care. The standard is one of reasonableness, and an action for abandonment will not generally lie when sufficient grounds for termination exist, along with reasonable efforts on the part of the physician to find alternative care.

CHAPTER TWO

NEGLIGENCE–BASED CLAIMS

I. IN GENERAL: THE STANDARD OF CARE

Negligence, the most common theory of liability in medical malpractice litigation, is defined as "conduct which falls below the standard established by law for the protection of others against unreasonable risk of harm." Restatement (Second) of Torts § 282 (1965). The negligence cause of action generally requires that four elements be established: (1) that an actor owes a duty of care to another; (2) that the applicable standard for carrying out the duty be breached; (3) that as a proximate cause of the breach of duty a compensable injury results; and (4) that there be compensable damages or injury to the plaintiff. The burden is on the plaintiff to establish each element of the negligence action by a preponderance of the evidence.

The standard of conduct that is required to meet the obligation of "due care" is based upon what the "reasonable practitioner" would do in like circumstances. The standard is not one of excellence or superior practice; it only requires that the physician exercise that degree of skill and care that would be expected of the average qualified practitioner practicing under like circumstances. Such circumstances might include the community in which the practitioner conducts his practice or the school of medicine to which he adheres. Thus, in a particular case, if two or more alternative procedures might have been used and the defendant selected one, the issue is whether a competent physician would have done so, even if another would not. The standard is also not one of good faith. The fact that a physician meant well or practiced to the best of his ability is not relevant. Conduct is always measured by objective criteria in terms of how the reasonable practitioner would perform under like circumstances.

The use of objective criteria is not, however, without its limits. Conduct involving professional skills and services is generally evaluated by standards determined by the profession; therefore what is objectively "right" does not always yield to consensus. Courts have not been entirely uniform in establishing the criteria that define a standard of care in any particular circumstance. Both courts and legislatures have, at various times, issued pronouncements about the standard of care for medical malpractice actions. Following the ruling of the Washington Supreme Court in *Helling v. Carey* (Wash.1974) in which the court specifically rejected evidence by uncontradicted testimony of the applicable professional standard and instead imposed its own, the Washington legislature responded immediately. It enacted a law that declared professional standards would henceforth be established by the profession and courts were not free to reject such standards.

A. RESPECTABLE MINORITY RULE

One such limit of objective criteria concerns standards and procedures that are adopted on a day-to-day basis within the practice of medicine. In a profession as complicated as medicine, physicians often do not agree on the therapeutic approach that ought to be used in a particular case. Indeed, the entire concept of "second opinions" arose in recognition of different methods of approach to medical care. The fact that a practitioner chooses a particular method that ultimately yields a poor result does not lead to the conclusion that a poor method was chosen. In acknowledging that medical approaches to treatment do vary and that courts are incapable of evaluating those kinds of judgments, most courts have adopted some sort of "respectable minority" test. In essence, the theory is that certain procedures, which might not be adopted by a majority of practicing physicians, might still be acceptable to a "respectable minority" of such practitioners. Thus, if a choice can be made among various alternative approaches to treating a particular condition and a respectable minority of physicians would have selected one such procedure, a physician will not be held liable for malpractice, assuming reasonable skill and care were exercised in providing such care.

A Texas court modified the "respectable minority" standard to reflect a better approach to this matter in *Henderson v. Heyer–Schulte Corp.* (Tex. Civ.App.1980). In *Henderson,* a physician performed a breast augmentation procedure that resulted in silicone leakage and movement throughout the patient's body. There was evidence that various qualified and respected members of the profession used the particular technique in the past. The court held that the issue was not whether a "respectable minority" or "considerable number" of physicians practice a particular technique, but whether the procedure meets a minimal threshold of due care as determined by the "average qualified physician" standard.

B. SCHOOL AND LOCALITY RULES

The standard of care that is applicable to a particular physician has historically depended, at least in part, on where he practices and what "school" of treatment he follows. The so-called "school rule" is largely a historical reference to the days when there existed different recognized schools of treatment. For example, the homeopathic and allopathic schools differed in that the latter, but not the former, used agents that caused different effects than those supposedly causing the disease. A practitioner from one school would not be expected to use a technique from another school. Contemporary examples include osteopaths and chiropractors and the theory remains that a practitioner from one school should only be held accountable according to the standards propounded by that school. In some states osteopaths are not permitted to prescribe drugs or perform surgical procedures. In these states, osteopaths are only held to the standard of care expected of osteopaths.

Even where they continue to exist, there are limits to the school rules. If, for instance, a patient voluntarily seeks the services of a chiropractor rather than orthopedist to treat a back problem, the patient may be reasonably expected to know that certain procedures, such as surgical intervention, will not be used. On the other hand, in *Mostrom v. Pettibon* (Wash.App.1980), a chiropractor was held liable for failing to identify and disclose that the patient had medical problems for which chiropractic treatment was inappropriate. The practical significance of school rules has largely been lost today as most practitioners are now held to the general standards of the medical profession.

As an adjunct to the school rule, physicians have also been held liable for their failure to recognize that a particular treatment issue was beyond their competence and should have been referred to a specialist for consultation and management. In *Pittman v. Gilmore* (5th Cir.1977), a general practitioner attempted to treat a patient who was reportedly coughing up blood for two days. The physician failed to appreciate the seriousness of the condition and did not refer the patient to a thoracic surgeon who might have been able to save the patient's life. The court held the general practitioner liable in negligence for failing to consult a specialist.

The standard of care expected of general practitioners and of specialists is another fertile area of litigation. In the typical case, a general practitioner that practices in a specific area of expertise, but refers patients to specialists when unable to manage a particular patient, will only be held to the standard of care of a generalist. A person who holds himself out as a specialist, however, is generally held to a higher standard of care. See *Shilkret v. Annapolis Emergency Hosp. Ass'n* (Md.1975). Even in those cases in which a practitioner is not a specialist, but performs services generally administered by a specialist, such practitioner may also be held to the higher standard of care.

A related area involves those practitioners that provide services in the allied health professions such as nursing, psychology, and other fields. The standard of care generally expected of these professionals is that which would be expected of the average qualified practitioner working in that field. If a practitioner holds himself out as possessing greater knowledge or expertise, he is likely to be held to the higher standard. In *Simpson v. Davis* (Kan.1976), a general dentist that performed endodontic work on a patient was held to the standard of a specialist because specialists generally performed those types of procedures.

The geographical location where a physician practices has historically had a bearing on the standard of care to which he is held. The "locality rule" was justified in two ways. First, physicians practicing in rural locations had less opportunity to learn how to perform new procedures or use new equipment, and had less access to modern facilities than their urban colleagues. For these reasons, it was considered unfair to hold them to the same standard of care as the urban practitioners that had much greater access to continuing medical education, new technologies, and superior facilities. Second, use of the locality rule was thought to create an incentive for physicians to practice in rural areas where there was often less opportunity to interact with and learn from colleagues, fewer patients to treat, and fewer patients with health insurance. Specialization, in particular, was more difficult in rural areas because the smaller patient population made it more difficult to support a practice.

The locality rule served primarily as a limitation on who could testify as an expert in a medical malpractice case. A physician outside of the same or similar locality would be precluded from testifying because his knowledge of the relevant medical standard for the particular community was considered inadequate. This was the "strict locality rule" and today it prevails only in a few jurisdictions.

In recent years courts have moved away from the kinds of geographical considerations that led to development of the locality rule. Recognizing that today's technological advances in transportation and the dissemination of information make it substantially easier for physicians in all locations to acquire the most current information and training, most states have moved away from the locality rule and instead are moving toward a more national standard of care. *See Hawes v. Chua* (D.C.App.2001) (maintaining expert testimony regarding a national standard of care must not be based on opinion, speculation, or conjecture, and must reflect some type of evidence indicative of a national standard of care, including national journals, meetings, or conventions). Many courts no longer view use of the locality rule as an incentive to attract physicians to rural locations, but instead consider it unjust. It is increasingly difficult to find physicians in rural areas that are willing to testify as experts, leading to the so-called "conspiracy of silence."

Today the geographic location of a malpractice defendant's practice is usually one factor to be considered by the jury, and it may have a bearing on the weight given to the testimony of an expert outside of the locality. However, it has less impact than it did half a century ago, and it usually does not preclude an expert from testifying as to the relevant community standard. The waning of the locality rule does not ignore the fact that regional variations in practice do exist or that the latest technology available in an urban area may not be available in a rural one. Thus in most states today, courts will hold that the applicable standard of care is that based upon practice in the "same or similar" location, with due regard for the state of medical science and the availability of certain knowledge and procedures at the time of the alleged malpractice. See *Henry v. Obstetrics and Gynecology Consultants*, (Tenn.App.2002) (maintaining expert testimony was inadmissible because doctor's knowledge did not occur until two years after the alleged malpractice and there was no testimony indicating it was applicable to the local or similar community). *See also Hall v. Hilbun* (Miss.1985); *Wall v. Stout* (N.C. 1984).

Those jurisdictions that retain some form of the locality rule defend it in a number of ways. Some argue that notwithstanding the advances in communication and travel, certain communities still have less access to state-of-the-art techniques and equipment. Others argue that the combination of both less specialized equipment and the absence of local specialists instructing on the use of new procedures makes it difficult for rural practitioners to really keep abreast of the technologies used by their urban counterparts. Furthermore, since actual parity is so difficult, it has been argued that the lesser standard is necessary to encourage practitioners to enter a practice in rural locations isolated from large medical centers.

The greatest concern today about using geographic frames of reference is the absence of standards to designate what constitutes a similar community for purposes of applying the locality rule. In general, a locality is considered to be similar to the one in question if it contains comparable medical facilities and practitioners have similar access to new knowledge about techniques and procedures. Because it is reasonable to allow the trier of fact to consider the nature of the facilities and equipment, as well as the availability of special equipment and more experienced physicians when necessary, the question of when a locality is similar to another becomes an important factor. In *Shilkret v. Annapolis Emergency Hosp. Ass'n* (Md.1975), the court essentially rejected the locality rule, noting that some courts look to geographic proximity while others consider demographic factors such as population, size and economic factors such as per capita income. Others, however, focus on medical factors such as the availability of research and laboratory facilities, teaching hospitals and modern equipment.

As a consequence of the concerns about the validity of locality rules, as well as the difficulties in application, many jurisdictions have either rejected the rule altogether or have subjected it to various limitations. For example, some courts have refused to apply geographic limitations on the standard of care that applies to specialists, instead requiring them to adhere to a standard applicable to specialists in general, and thus to keep abreast of national developments through whatever means are available to them. *See, e.g., Taylor v. Hill* (Me.1983). A number of courts have rejected the locality rule completely or have limited it to a single factor for the trier of fact to consider. *See Shilkret v. Annapolis Emergency Hosp. Ass'n, supra,* in which the court held that the standard should include "advances in the profession, availability of facilities, specialization or general practice, proximity of specialists and special facilities, together with all other relevant considerations...." Although courts are moving away from the locality rule, geographic considerations may continue to be asserted for some time. Even those courts that presently reject them are more likely to allow evidence of geographical considerations, but to give little weight to professional standards that are arguably different than a national standard.

C.   BEST JUDGMENT RULE

The question of whether in some cases the obligation of a physician is to adhere not only to the standard of the "average qualified practitioner" but to some higher standard is a difficult one. If, in a certain situation, a physician believes the acceptable medical practice to be unreasonably dangerous and he has sufficient expertise to know of a better practice, does he have an obligation to use his superior knowledge and skill? If so, can he be held accountable if he fails to do so? Of course, if the practitioner adheres to a standard of care that is inferior to that of the average qualified practitioner, he is not shielded from liability on the basis that he exercised his best judgment.

There is case law to support the proposition that a practitioner with superior skill or knowledge has a duty to exercise a higher standard, making him accountable in negligence if he fails to do so. The principle was first articulated in *Toth v. Cmty. Hosp. at Glen Cove* (N.Y.1968). In that case, a pediatrician treating dangerously ill premature twins recommended a course of action that was intended to keep them alive and prevent brain damage. Although there was evidence that this treatment constituted accepted medical practice at the time, there was new evidence that indicated that such treatment was of little value and imposed an unnecessary risk of irreversible eye damage, which did in fact occur. The court held that "evidence that the defendant followed customary practice is not the sole test of professional malpractice," noting "if a physician fails to employ his expertise or best judgment . . . he should not automatically be freed from liability because he adhered to acceptable practice." Rather, "a physician would use his best judgment and whatever superior knowledge, skill and intelligence he has."

In a subsequent New York case examining nearly the same issue, a pediatric resident prescribed a certain level of oxygen for a premature infant that was consistent with good medical care. A pediatric instructor who was allegedly studying the effects of increased oxygen on such babies countermanded his order, however. Although the baby had been doing well on the conventional treatment, the instructor increased the dosage of oxygen because the study called for the conventional treatment on one out of every three infants, and increased the oxygen for two of the three. The increased oxygen ultimately proved dangerous, and a lawsuit against the instructor followed. In finding liability on behalf of the instructor, the court stated:

> Without in any way challenging the legitimacy of the debate . . . as to the effect of the curtailment of oxygen on premature infants, we find it difficult to believe that any reputable institution

would permit two out of three patients to receive unusual treatment, which might result in death or brain damage, unless it was fairly convinced that the conventional wisdom no longer applied.... Dr. Engle and the hospital cannot avail themselves of the shield of acceptable medical practice....

Burton v. Brooklyn Doctors Hosp. (N.Y.A.D.1982). The difficulty in applying the "best judgment rule" arises in those cases in which a new treatment, potentially better than the industry standard, also exposes the patient to certain risks. If one of the risks materializes, the physician may subject himself to liability for failure to adhere to the professional standard. Certain safeguards, such as the "respectable minority" rule and the "error in judgment" rule, offer some protection to practitioners that treat patients through exercise of their best judgment. Although there is potential for a practitioner to be held legally liable for using his best judgment, this risk is decreased if the practitioner limits his best judgment to procedures that do not subject the patient to additional risk.

II. PROVING THE PROFESSIONAL STANDARD

The vast majority of medical malpractice cases require proof of negligence that is secured through expert testimony. Because it is usually difficult, if not virtually impossible, for lay jurors to determine both the appropriate standard of care and whether or not it has been violated, the assistance of expert testimony is critical. With the burden of proof and persuasion resting with the plaintiff, the plaintiff must usually offer expert testimony or risk a directed verdict for the defendant.

The difficulty that a plaintiff faces in securing expert testimony should not be understated. A "conspiracy of silence" is thought to exist among practitioners, particularly those in small, rural locations. This "conspiracy" refers to physicians' reluctance to testify against one another in malpractice actions. This issue is thought to arise in part because of a fear that the colleague may retaliate, particularly the next time the "expert" becomes a defendant. There is also the concern that physicians who become involved in legal matters may not get referrals from other colleagues or even insurers. Perhaps the greatest justification for the "conspiracy of silence" however, is that physicians feel that it is morally objectionable and disloyal to testify against "one's own". Plaintiffs can be forced to use so-called "hired guns" when they are otherwise unable to find a physician to testify as an expert. Hired guns are physicians that make a practice of getting involved in litigation, often testifying in many different cases, serving as an expert witness. Often they attempt to testify in a variety of cases, even without a genuine expertise in a particular field. In recent years the standards concerning qualification of expert witnesses have made it more difficult for "hired guns" to participate in cases for which they have little expertise.

In contrast to the difficulties often experienced by malpractice plaintiffs in finding suitable and willing expert witnesses, defendants are generally much more successful in finding agreeable colleagues who will come to their defense. Physicians asked to participate in litigation on behalf of defendants may still be reluctant, but generally they object to the time-consuming nature of the practice, particularly being available for trial at unpredictable times, and have an overall dislike of the litigation process. Today many courts have addressed the burdensome nature of the legal process by allowing videotaped expert testimony when appropriate. Defendants generally are able to find suitable expert testimony without significant difficulty.

A. COMPETENCY OF EXPERTS

Practitioners that are called upon to serve as expert witnesses are generally required to be knowledgeable, and preferably experienced, in the appropriate standard of care for which they are testifying. For an expert to be considered knowledgeable, the expert must have a general knowledge about the standard of care to be applied under the circumstances. In addition, if the jurisdiction adheres to any form of the locality rule, the expert must be familiar with the standard practices for the particular location. This does not mean that the witness must necessarily be of the same specialty as the defendant or that he even necessarily follow the same school of medicine. In *Bartimus v. Paxton*

Cmty. Hosp. (Ill.App.1983), the court was willing to qualify a physician to testify against an osteopath, assuming that he could demonstrate sufficient familiarity with the standards of osteopathy.

Courts are generally willing to find that a specialist is capable of testifying about the standard of care expected of a general practitioner. The reverse, however, is not necessarily true. A general practitioner may or may not be qualified to testify against a specialist, even if he claims to be familiar with the applicable standards. *See Taylor v. Hill* (Me.1983) (permitting the testimony). Some courts have held that general practitioners are *per se* disqualified to testify against specialists, regardless of their demonstrated familiarity with the necessary standard of care. *See Tate v. Detroit Receiving Hosp.* (Mich.App. 2002) (maintaining that experts must specialize in the same specialty that the defendant physician was practicing during the alleged malpractice, at the same time as the alleged malpractice, in order to testify as an expert). A court typically requires that the purported expert is familiar with the applicable standard of care and that he is able to determine whether there is a causal connection between a violation of that standard and the injuries that are presented.

The testimonial competence of witnesses offered as experts is a matter that is handled in one of two ways by the trial courts. Most courts require a potential expert to establish a minimum threshold of competence before he may testify. The first part of an expert's testimony will establish his credentials and any other matters that bear upon his ability to offer an "expert" opinion. Many courts, after taking evidence on that issue, possibly after cross-examination, will provisionally "qualify" the expert to testify. If the court declines to qualify the expert, he would not be permitted to testify further. The court's decision about the threshold qualification of experts is determined by applicable statute or case law.

The alternative to requiring a threshold inquiry about whether a particular expert is qualified to testify is to wait and see what the expert is asked to comment on. On that basis a court will determine whether he is qualified to do so. The determination about whether an expert is competent is one generally made by the court, whereas the weight that will be accorded to that testimony is generally a matter for the jury. In a few jurisdictions, there are statutory requirements concerning the qualification of expert witnesses.

The determination of whether a witness offered as an expert is competent to testify is generally made on the basis of two factors: whether he is familiar with the course of treatment in question (including its purpose, contraindications, risks and alternatives) and whether he is familiar with the relevant professional standard at the time the procedure was adopted. This determination is made after the plaintiff lays a foundation for the expert testimony, and has an opportunity to demonstrate that a proposed witness has sufficient expertise to qualify as an expert. The trial judge has the exclusive discretion to evaluate these factors.

The fact that an expert claims to have the necessary familiarity is not conclusive. In *Gilmore v. O'Sullivan* (Mich.App.1981), a proposed expert in obstetrics and gynecology was not permitted to testify as an expert in a case involving prenatal care and delivery of an infant. Finding that the physician was not board-certified in obstetrics and gynecology and that there was insufficient evidence of practical and research experience, the court refused to qualify him as an expert witness. Although occupational experience used to be a traditional requirement, (see *Reinhardt v. Colton* (Minn.1983)), courts today are more flexible in their determination of what constitutes familiarity with professional standards. Thus, a physician that has the necessary experience in the general field and sufficient basic training may still qualify as an expert.

B.   EXCEPTIONS TO THE NEED FOR EXPERT TESTIMONY

The difficulty that plaintiffs experience in locating competent experts to testify on their behalf is only one reason that expert testimony is sometimes impractical. Another is the expense involved. Physicians often charge a premium for their willingness to serve as an expert witness. In order to render an opinion, the expert must acquire substantial familiarity with the plaintiff's case and surrounding circumstances. Usually he must issue a report and often he will submit to a deposition. All of this is required even before trial. Insurance does not pay for litigation. Even if a case is being handled on a contingency basis, the expert costs accrue and often must be paid up front, regardless of whether there is a favorable outcome. Many meritorious cases are never pursued merely because of the prohibitive cost of expert witnesses. As a result, great attention has been paid in recent years to finding ways of pursuing a medical malpractice case without the need for expert testimony.

1. Defendant's Own Testimony

Unlike criminal defendants who can assert the "Fifth Amendment", thus invoking their privilege not to testify against themselves, civil defendants have no comparable right. There is nothing that prevents the plaintiff from calling the defendant physician on behalf of the plaintiff and requiring that he testify to facts that are within his own knowledge. Here he acts as a "percipient" or "fact" witness and whatever testimony the plaintiff can elicit from him is valid and usable. The question of whether, additionally, he must also be willing to provide expert testimony is a more difficult one. The old rule was usually that a defendant not be so required because to do so would be unfair. In recent years, however, courts, sensitive to the difficulties of plaintiffs in securing medical experts, have been more willing to allow enough inquiry of the defendant to establish the requisite standard of care. In *McDermott v. Manhattan Eye, Ear and Throat*

Hosp. (N.Y.1964), the appellate court reversed the trial court's exclusion of the plaintiff's questioning of the defendant physician as to the applicable standard of care in his field on the basis of a textbook that he had written on the subject. Recognizing the difficulty in providing expert testimony, the court noted, "the plaintiff's only recourse in many cases may be to question the defendant doctor ... in the hope that he will thereby be able to establish his malpractice claim. There is nothing unfair about such a practice."

Assuming that the defendant can be required to testify as an expert in his own case, the value of such testimony is still a critical issue. Obviously there is no guarantee that his expert "opinion" will be consistent with proving the plaintiff's case. More likely, he will make every effort to sabotage it. Even if books and treatises are introduced, he will most likely attempt to minimize their value or their relevance to the case. As a result, it is clearly better strategy to have other means of establishing the essential elements of the plaintiff's case and to rely on testimony or admissions of the defendant to the least extent possible.

A significant testimonial matter arises when a defendant is called as an expert witness. An expert witness is not initially an adverse, or "hostile" one, and the rule that generally allows adverse witnesses to be interrogated through leading questions and impeached by their own testimony is not necessarily applicable. The modern trend, however, is to recognize an opposing party as an adverse witness and allow him to be examined as such.

Yet another difficult matter is determining whether a physician's out-of-court statements that are admissible as exceptions to the hearsay rule may be used in lieu of expert testimony. In *Wickoff v. James* (Cal.App.1958), the plaintiff's husband overheard the defendant admit to another physician, "boy, I made a mess of things." Furthermore, he admitted to the husband that he had severed the patient's intestine while inserting a sigmoidoscope into the patient's rectum. The court held that these statements constituted admissions against interest and that they were sufficient to serve in lieu of expert testimony.

2. Common Knowledge

A second potential means of avoiding the expert testimony requirement is through use of the "common knowledge" doctrine. The common knowledge doctrine can be invoked when: (1) the defendant's "negligence is gross", (2) "the medical condition is obvious," or (3)"the plaintiff's evidence of injury creates a probability so strong that a lay juror can form a reasonable belief." *Gordon v. Glass* (Conn. App.2001). Thus if the fact finder can call upon his own knowledge and wisdom and apply a suitable standard of care without the aid of expert testimony, the plaintiff may be entitled to a ruling that expert testimony is not required. For example, a patient who undergoes a mastectomy on the wrong breast does not require the testimony of an expert to persuade the jury that the action constitutes malpractice. In *Killingsworth v. Poon* (Ga.App. 1983), the common knowledge doctrine was invoked to demonstrate that the defendant, who injected the patient in the shoulder, was liable in negligence for a resulting puncture to the patient's lung. *See also Schwartz v. Abay* (Kan.App.1999) (holding no need for expert testimony to establish claim of negligence when doctor admitted to operating on and removing part of the patient's wrong vertebral disc). Similarly, in *Cangemi v. Cone* (Pa.Super.Ct.2001), the court concluded that expert testimony was not required to establish the negligence of either a physician or a hospital for the resulting death of a patient, when an x-ray clearly disclosed an aneurysm, but the patient was released from the hospital before anyone reviewed the x-ray. The court maintained that the failure to review an available report that indicated a serious medical condition was so obviously indicative of lack of due care that no expert testimony was necessary to establish negligence.

The current trend in malpractice cases among some courts has been to expand the scope of cases in which common knowledge allows a case to overcome a directed verdict and make it to the jury. For example, in *Pry v. Jones* (Ark.1972), the court allowed common knowledge to let a case go to the jury in which it was alleged that the plaintiff's ureter was severed while she underwent a hysterectomy. Although there was also evidence that the procedure was complicated and by its nature it required an incision in close proximity to the ureter, the case was nevertheless permitted to go to the jury with "common knowledge" in lieu of expert testimony.

In other cases, however, courts have not been as generous in allowing the jury to consider common knowledge as to negligence without expert testimony. In *Ward v. Levy & Unger* (Mass.App.1989), the plaintiff allegedly suffered a facial injury during a tooth extraction. An offer of proof was made consisting only of the patient's own affidavit, medical records and photographs and a letter from the surgeon treating the facial injury. No evidence was offered on the causal connection between the alleged negligence and the injury. The court held that common knowledge was not sufficient to establish that link and that a jury would be left to conjecture without expert testimony. This case seems to demonstrate the inherent difficulty in small cases: a laceration on the face may have occurred on the basis of the defendant's negligence yet the small extent of damages will probably not warrant the expense of a medical expert.

Another recent case demonstrates that common knowledge is reserved for only those instances in which it would be obvious to a lay jury that an injury resulted from professional negligence. In *Evanston Hosp. v. Crane* (Ill.App.1993), the plaintiff, who failed to submit an expert affidavit in a summary judgment proceeding, claimed that he should have been referred to a cardiologist because he was diagnosed with a heart condition. He further contended that it was in the common knowledge of a layperson to make such a judgment. The court rejected his claim, holding that whether a patient should be referred to a specialist is not properly resolved by the common knowledge of a layperson.

3. Violation of a Statute

When a defendant violates a civil or criminal statute, ordinance or regulation, and the plaintiff claims that the violation is causally related to his injuries, such violation might support an allegation of negligence, even without expert testimony. In these cases, two issues must be resolved. First, it must be determined if the statute or regulation is intended both to protect persons such as the plaintiff and to prevent the type of injury that the plaintiff allegedly sustained. Without a sufficient causal connection, the mere fact that a regulation was violated does not obviate the need for expert testimony. Second, it must be determined what procedural effect the violation should be given.

In a situation in which these requirements are satisfied, the violation of the statute is considered to be "negligence *per se*" or "statutory negligence" and expert testimony may not be required to establish negligence. *Landeros v. Flood* (Cal.1976) illustrates this principle. In *Landeros*, an 11–month old baby was brought to the emergency room suffering from an injury that seemed to have been inflicted by a twisting action. No explanation was given for the injury. The physician failed to diagnose battered child syndrome, and also failed to perform an x-ray on the child's head, which would have revealed a skull fracture. The child was discharged to his mother's home, where he was severely injured again. The purpose of an existing statute, which requires mandatory reporting of child abuse, is to protect children at risk from further injury. A resulting lawsuit was permitted on the basis that the physician breached his statutory duty to report the child's injuries, and that further injury ensued.

Violation of a statute can be alleged in the plaintiff's case, even if it does not preclude the need for expert testimony. In such a case, the procedural effect will likely not be that an expert needs to testify, but rather that the violation may bear upon the standard of care and be introduced as part of the plaintiff's prima facie case. Assuming that a violation of a statute is found, it is not necessarily true that the violation conclusively establishes negligence. Some courts maintain that such a violation establishes a rebuttable presumption of negligence. In those cases the plaintiff is not initially entitled to a directed verdict, but may later get one if the defendant is not able to rebut the presumption of negligence. A majority of courts hold that violations of a statute result in evidence of negligence, noting that it is up to the jury to determine what weight the evidence should be given.

An example of those cases in which violation of a statute is not necessarily probative of negligence is when a licensing statute is allegedly violated. If a practitioner is found to be practicing without a license and commits an act of alleged negligence, is the absence of a license probative on the issue of whether the act was negligent? According to *McCarthy v. Boston City Hosp.* (Mass.1971), the answer seems to depend upon whether the absence of a license was due to a determination on the part of the licensing authority that the practitioner was not fit to practice, or whether it amounted to some sort of oversight. In *McCarthy*, the physician's absence of a license occurred as a result of a lapse in his registration. It did not appear, however, that it in any way affected the quality of his patient care. The court held that the absence of a license was not the proximate cause of the patient's injury.

In those cases in which the absence of a license results from the license being revoked, suspended or never obtained, it is more likely to be probative on the issue of competence to practice, whether or not an actual causal connection is found. In *Stahlin v. Hilton Hotels Corp.* (7th Cir.1973), violation of a statute was held to be probative when a nurse violated the Nursing Act by practicing without a license. The court determined that the practitioner did not have the qualifications required of nurses and thus was not competent to perform the services that led to the claim of malpractice.

4. Medical Literature and Manufacturers' Instructions

The question of whether medical literature might be used in lieu of a medical expert depends, initially, upon whether the literature is even admissible and upon what probative value it will be given. The general rule is that most literature is not admissible to prove the truth of what it contains because it constitutes hearsay. *See generally,* 84 A.L.R.2d 1338 (1962, Supp.1979, 1984). There is an exception, however, recognized by the Federal Rules of Evidence (see Fed. R. Evid. Rule 803 (18)) and by a growing number of states (see West's Mass. Gen. Laws Ann. ch. 233, § 79C). The exception recognizes medical literature, including treatises, as reliable authority within the profession. Such literature can either be introduced on direct examination of an expert who relies on it or is asked to comment upon it in his testimony, or it can be introduced during cross-examination of an expert who is asked to comment upon its reliability as well as its content.

The common objection to use of medical literature, particularly in lieu of experts, is the lack of opportunity for cross-examination. The author of such a text does not appear in court; therefore, he or she cannot be cross-examined. Nor can the text be examined as to how individual variations that exist in actual cases affect the conclusions in the treatise. Furthermore, the effect of treatises on a lay jury is uncertain. Some jurors are unable to understand them and as a consequence tend to discount the evidence. Others do just the opposite, giving undue deference merely because it appears as published literature. Because many medical techniques and procedures are time-sensitive, it is not always possible to determine what the standard of practice was at a given time. A particular passage may be written two to three years before the date of publication.

There is also the problem that different medical literature may be favorable to different parties' cases. What happens if there is contrary literature introduced? Credibility is usually determined on the basis of observation of demeanor of the person testifying. Juries have little ability to assess the credibility of conflicting treatises or to understand the reasons for differing opinions on a particular subject. In these cases medical literature is generally not relied upon in lieu of an expert, but is only used to bolster the credibility of an expert who is able to present the treatise and testify about its reliability and relevance to the case.

The question arises as to whether medical literature, in and of itself, is probative enough for establishing a medical fact that it is sufficient to get to the jury. The answer seems to be that it would be difficult to offer the treatise in evidence without a medical "expert" to comment upon its validity in a particular case. When the purpose of the literature is to preclude the need for an expert, the "expert" called upon is generally the defendant himself. Thus if it appears that there is a treatise on point and that the defendant will establish the relevance and reliability of the treatise, the final hurdle is to establish on the basis of any admissions in prior testimony (e.g., by deposition) that the testimony, along with the treatise, is sufficient to get to the jury.

Information provided by product manufacturers is handled differently. The type of information that may be contained in a package insert of a drug, for example, contains warnings, side effects, and contraindications for use. The Food and Drug Administration (FDA) requires that all drugs, unless otherwise exempt, be approved for patient use. It also requires that prescription drugs be packaged with an informational insert that describes the drug and gives a detailed explanation of its use. Other items prepared with manufacturer's instructions have been the subject of malpractice litigation, particularly on the issue of how the manufacturer's information affects the standard of care.

In those jurisdictions that recognize an exception to the hearsay rule for medical literature generally, the same exception applies to material contained in the package inserts. This is due to the fact that nearly the same information is reiterated in the Physicians' Desk Reference (PDR), a publication that contains extensive information about drug products and is considered to be a reliable source. Even in those jurisdictions that do not recognize this hearsay exception, a package insert may constitute admissible evidence, if offered for a reason other than for the truth of the information contained within it. If the issue is whether the physician should have been on notice of a contraindication in the use of a particular product, for example, the package insert may be probative on that issue.

Medical literature, treatises and package inserts are the typical types of evidence that experts will bring into court and rely upon while they are testifying. Only on rare occasion might a court permit a research study to be admitted in evidence. In *Young v. Horton* (Mont.1993), the court admitted a number of journal articles in a case in which the plaintiff denied that she had given consent to surgery. The articles suggested that patients frequently forget when their consent involves a surgical procedure.

The question of whether manufacturers' literature such as a package insert, in and of itself, is sufficient to get to the jury is a difficult one. Clearly in conjunction with a testifying expert, the insert, assuming admissibility, can provide valuable information. If the defendant will provide the "expert" testimony, the package insert or other manufacturers' literature can assist in proving the plaintiff's case. Further, if the common knowledge doctrine is otherwise applicable, the manufacturer's literature in conjunction with common knowledge should generally suffice. Whether a manufacturer's literature without common knowledge is sufficient to get to the jury is still a difficult question. The case law is sparse and conflicting. In *Ohligschlager v. Proctor Cmty. Hosp.* (Ill.1973), the court suggested that the literature provided by the manufacturer might be adequate in a liability case against a physician to get beyond a directed verdict. However, in a subsequent case, *Mielke v. Condell Mem'l Hosp.* (Ill.App. 1984), the holding in *Ohligschlager* was limited to physicians. As to a standard of care expected of hospitals, manufacturers' literature alone was not sufficient to get to the jury.

The reasons that plaintiffs attempt to use manufacturers literature in lieu of medical experts is generally the same as for the use of the common knowledge doctrine: medical experts are difficult to obtain and either too expensive for cases that do not warrant expert fees or the plaintiff is simply unable to afford them. When the information contained in this literature is on point it becomes a valuable source of timely and accurate information. However, it is also important to ensure that the literature is relevant and material to the case, as well as understandable to a lay jury. This means that the literature must actually reflect the state of knowledge and practice in the profession, and not some ideal standard that is not actually practiced. The defendant, of course, is entitled to contradict the evidence and demonstrate that it is not consistent with the industry standard. That does not affect the literature's admissibility, however, unless it tends to deviate so far as to vitiate its probative value.

5. Res Ipsa Loquitur

Probably the largest exception to the requirement that plaintiffs bear the burden of proof in establishing liability is advanced in those cases in which there is little direct evidence of negligence, but there is significant indirect or circumstantial evidence. Known as "res ipsa loquitur," or literally, "the thing speaks for itself," this doctrine is invoked in cases where negligence can only be estab-

lished by drawing an inference from the circumstances. Generally these circumstances include a
mishap for which there is no credible explanation
and which does not usually occur in the absence of
someone being negligent.

The seminal case establishing the applicability of
res ipsa loquitur was the English case *Byrne v.
Boadle* (Eng.Rep.1863). In *Byrne*, the plaintiff was
hit in the head by a barrel of flour while walking
down the street. The barrel fell from the window of
a warehouse that was owned by the defendant. The
court invoked the doctrine of res ipsa loquitur,
holding that in the absence of negligence, barrels of
flour do not generally fall out of windows.

The res ipsa doctrine is largely intact today. In an
applicable case, its effect is to shift the burden of
proof to the defendant to explain why he was not
negligent and, in the absence of a credible explanation, to permit, but not require, the jury to infer
negligence. Some courts prefer to explain the effect
of res ipsa loquitur as establishing the plaintiff's
prima facie case of negligence, and thus the case
goes to the jury on that basis.

The application of the doctrine to medical malpractice cases has been with some reservation. Often it is applied to those cases in which a mishap
occurs while a patient is unconscious or otherwise
unable to determine why there was a particular
occurrence. It is not intended to make the physician
an insurer of a particular result, nor is it intended
to create liability on the part of the physicians

merely because a bad outcome results. Res ipsa is thus not applicable when any known or perceived risk to a certain procedure occurs. It is reserved solely for those unexplained occurrences that generally do not happen in the absence of negligence.

In order for a court to apply the res ipsa loquitur doctrine, the following conditions generally must be satisfied: (1) the subject matter must be within the common knowledge of a lay person, (2) the defendant must have the exclusive control over the instrumentality causing the damage, (3) the event would not normally occur in the absence of negligence, and (4) the plaintiff did not voluntarily contribute to the occurrence. *Brown v. Baptist Mem'l Hosp.* (Miss.2002). The availability of res ipsa loquitur for a particular situation is a matter for the discretion of the trial court. Most courts employing this doctrine allow a permissive inference of negligence. The permissive inference of negligence is not tantamount to a presumption, rebuttable or conclusive. The jury is free to accept or reject the inference, and thus no evidence on behalf of the defendant is required for a verdict for the defendant. The only clear procedural effect is that the plaintiff can rest, even without introducing expert testimony on the issue of causation, and the case will still go to the jury.

The purpose behind the res ipsa doctrine is to assist patients who sustain some sort of injury or adverse consequence of a medical procedure for which it was impossible for them to know what might have happened to cause the injury. The most difficult part of sustaining the burden of demon-strating the applicability of res ipsa is showing that the mishap does not generally occur in the absence of negligence. This is not an "expert" standard; it is something to be determined by the average person in light of ordinary experience and as a consequence of common knowledge. Among the most common situations in which res ipsa has been invoked are those cases alleging that a medical instrument or sponge was left inside a patient during surgery.

The application of res ipsa loquitur does not negate the need to establish causation in a case in which it is invoked. It will likely assist in establish-ing fault by use of circumstantial evidence that is probative of causation, but the burden of proof on the causation issue still remains initially with the plaintiff. As a result, expert testimony is sometimes used to help meet the elements of the res ipsa doctrine. In *Hale v. Venuto* (Cal.App.1982) the plaintiff suffered peroneal and tibial palsy in her foot after undergoing surgery on her kneecap to correct a dislocation. The plaintiff produced expert testimony that suggested that the injury was proba-bly a result of negligence. On appeal, the court allowed application of the res ipsa doctrine, even though there had been adequate expert testimony on the issue of causation. The court reached its conclusion on the basis of all of the evidence, in-cluding the common knowledge doctrine.

Some courts broadly construe the requirement that the defendant have exclusive control of the instrumentality that apparently caused the injury.

In the landmark case *Ybarra v. Spangard* (Cal. 1944), the plaintiff underwent an appendectomy, only to later experience sharp pain in his right shoulder. He subsequently suffered atrophy and eventual paralysis of the shoulder muscles. The patient sued all of the health care providers that were present during the procedure, including the anesthesiologist, the primary and consulting surgeons, as well as number of other hospital employees, including the owner of the hospital. Although it was likely that at least some of the defendants were not negligent, the purpose of the res ipsa doctrine is to infer that there was negligence by any or all of them, making it incumbent upon them to come forward and explain what happened. The hope is that if res ipsa is invoked against all of them, each will be encouraged to reveal what he/she knows. Without res ipsa, each defendant could engage in a conspiracy of silence, and force the plaintiff to prove his own case.

The *Ybarra* court permitted use of res ipsa, even though it was clear that not all defendants had actual control over the patient. Rather, the court held that the test was a "right of control" and that under that standard each defendant had the burden of explaining the cause of the patient's injury. The court justified its departure from the traditional res ipsa limitations by explaining that the special relationship between physician and patient requires that those to whom the patient entrusted his care assume responsibility for the mishap.

The requirement that the plaintiff demonstrate that he did not, in any way, contribute to his own injury is generally the least difficult part of the plaintiff's burden. Often patients are anesthetized when the injury occurs and generally they have entrusted their care to the physician. Patients do decline medical care, elect among alternative procedures and sometimes act against medical advice. In so doing, they can bring about a medical condition or exacerbate an existing one. They generally do not, however, voluntarily cause a mishap while under the exclusive care of a physician. Thus if the first three elements of res ipsa are satisfied, the fourth element, the absence of contributory negligence, is usually satisfied as well.

Res ipsa also has both statutory and practical limitations. Under North Dakota law, for example, the doctrine is not applicable in medical malpractice cases unless the breach is so egregious that it would amount to common knowledge that a layman would comprehend. In *Maguire v. Taylor* (8th Cir.1991), the doctrine was held not to apply to a case involving nerve damage since it was beyond the basic understanding of lay jurors to determine whether it could happen in the absence of negligence.

Courts also differ on whether the court or the jury should decide whether the basic elements of the res ipsa doctrine have been satisfied. Some courts hold that if the plaintiff's case meets a certain threshold (i.e., "reasonable minds can differ") the jury is left to determine whether the elements have been proved. See *Sammons v. Smith* (Iowa

1984). Others hold that the court should determine whether the elements of res ipsa are satisfied and, if they have been, then the jury should evaluate all of the evidence and determine the procedural effect of applying the doctrine.

Assuming that it is determined that res ipsa is applicable, the usual consequence is that the case goes to the jury with the instruction that they may infer that the plaintiff's injury resulted from negligence, but they are not required to do so. Courts differ, however, on how they treat plaintiffs' expert testimony that is used to support the inference of negligence. Traditionally, if the plaintiff needs to use expert testimony to support their case, the doctrine of res ipsa is not applicable. Res ipsa is reserved for those cases in which the common knowledge of lay jurors is adequate to support the inference. See *Marquis v. Battersby* (Ind.App.1982). Unless the expert testimony was completely unnecessary, it removed the case from one fitting into the "common knowledge" exception, to one requiring the use of expert testimony.

The current trend seems to be toward expanding the availability of res ipsa and allowing it to be applied both in "common knowledge" cases in which the inference can be made exclusively by the lay juror, and in those cases where expert testimony is supplied to support the inference. See *Horner v. Northern Pac. Beneficial Ass'n Hosps., Inc.* (Wash. 1963). Under this view the purpose of the res ipsa doctrine is to yield a permissive inference of negligence in those cases in which the elements can be established, by any available means. Thus the use of expert testimony to support the common knowledge exception, leading to an inference of negligence, would not render the doctrine inapplicable. Res ipsa is not merely a facet of the "common knowledge" exception. Res ipsa is a separate doctrine that allows the use of circumstantial evidence when the necessary prerequisites are satisfied.

Not surprisingly, in a number of cases in which res ipsa would probably be persuasive, plaintiffs have still been reluctant to rely upon it. If the court finds that the doctrine is not applicable, the absence of a liability expert would likely be fatal to the case. As a result, it is common today to invoke res ipsa in addition to supplying expert testimony to increase the certainty that liability will be established. Particularly in those jurisdictions where the presence of expert testimony does not render res ipsa inapplicable, it is common to plead in the alternative: specific acts of negligence as demonstrated by the expert testimony, and res ipsa as to those acts for which it is not clear how they may have occurred. *See Reilly v. Straub* (Iowa 1979). In other courts, however, the pleading of specific acts of negligence precludes resort to the res ipsa doctrine because the primary source of evidence will not be circumstantial. *See Gilbert v. Middlesex Hosp.* (Conn.App.2000). In *Gilbert*, the court maintained that the jury was not entitled to an instruction on the doctrine of res ipsa loquitur because the plaintiff introduced the testimony of a medical expert to support her claim that the physicians that left a sponge inside her body after she gave birth were negligent. In order to properly use res ipsa, the court required that the plaintiff rely only on circumstantial evidence.

Finally, a few courts have added an additional element to the prerequisites for invoking res ipsa. Some courts require that the defendant be in a better position than the plaintiff to determine the cause of plaintiff's injury. If, for example, the plaintiff was anesthetized when the injury occurred, this condition would likely be met. *Horner, supra.* If, however, an injury occurs but the circumstances surrounding the injury unclear, application of the doctrine is more unlikely because it would probably require an expert to establish causation. It is difficult however to imagine a case in which the basic res ipsa elements are met, but the defendant was not be in a better position than the plaintiff to determine the cause of the injury.

The consequence of the permissive inference that res ipsa yields is to permit the jury to determine the overall credibility of the plaintiff's case in light of the evidence, testimony and cross-examination of the witnesses. It does not require that the jury accept the permissive inference allowed by the doctrine. It also does not affect the credibility of the defendant's evidence or overall presentation. Use of the res ipsa doctrine does not preclude the defendant from testifying that he conformed to the applicable standard of care, without offering an explanation for the plaintiff's injury. Without such an explanation, res ipsa does not necessarily mean that the plaintiff prevails. When a defendant testifies credibly that he did everything in his power to exercise due care, and the reason for the occurrence is unknown to him, the jury is entitled to find for the defendant, even if the res ipsa elements have been satisfied.

CHAPTER THREE

INTENTIONAL TORTS

I. IN GENERAL: HARM AND INTENT

As discussed in chapter 2, the predominant theory of liability in a medical malpractice action is negligence. Negligence connotes an unintended act that causes harm or, less commonly, an intended act that unintentionally causes harm. As the name suggests, an element of *intent* is required to prove intentional torts. In such actions the defendant is not necessarily alleged to have intentionally harmed the patient; rather, he intentionally acted in a fashion that ultimately caused harm to the patient. The practitioner's actions were not a consequence of mistake. Indeed, the practitioner expected the result that was achieved, but did not expect that the patient would later complain about his actions. Thus a medical procedure poorly performed might constitute negligence, while a medical procedure correctly performed that was not consented to might constitute an intentional tort.

Intentional torts strongly suggests that an element of "intent" accompanies the commission of the tort. Sometimes, however, the intent is inferred from the circumstances. For example, if informed consent is lacking, the elements of a battery may be established by inferring that there was an intention to act without consent. See infra at chapter 4. If intangible interests are affected (e.g., a right of privacy), the inference of intent may be satisfied by knowledge of the likely consequences of the action. Often intentional torts occur under conditions that the practitioner believes he has performed competently and rightly, only later to discover that his actions were tortious. Of course, in other situations, practitioners who commit intentional torts know of what they are doing, presumably believing that a lawsuit will not result.

The practical consequences of intentional torts are significant. First, the need for expert testimony generally required in a negligence action to establish the standard of care and the breach of that standard may be obviated. The critical element to prove is "intent" and expert testimony is usually not probative on that issue.

Secondly, a practitioner who is insured for his acts of negligence may find that his professional liability insurance policy disclaims coverage for intentional acts. A plaintiff often faces a serious dilemma when contemplating characterization of professional acts as intentional, thereby potentially cutting off the major source of payment of the claim.

Third, a claim may lie in intentional tort even if there is little or no damages. If, for example, a procedure was performed without the consent of the patient, no "harm" might have resulted; indeed the patient may be said to have benefited. Nevertheless, an action lies in intentional tort for the patient having been deprived of his right to choose, and the absence of tangible damages is not fatal to the claim as would be the case in a negligence action.

Finally, an intentional act may subject the defendant to criminal as well as civil liability in some cases. The same case alleging lack of informed consent and thus civil assault and battery claims could also result in criminal charges of assault and battery, if appropriate. In other cases of intentional tort, a psychiatrist who breaches his duty of care to a patient by engaging in a sexual relationship with the patient exposes himself not only to an action for intentional tort, but in some jurisdictions, criminal liability. Because of the procedural and evidentiary consequences (positive and negative) of pleading a case in intentional tort, often malpractice plaintiffs will plead their cases in both negligence and intentional tort, or in the alternative. If both theories are presented, somewhat different facts may support each theory. If they are presented in the alternative (which is permitted by some, but not all, courts) the same facts can support both theories and the jury is left to sort out which, if any, causes of action have been proved on the basis of the evidence.

A. ASSAULT AND BATTERY

A battery occurs when an individual is subjected to non-consensual touching that is in some way harmful or offensive to him. An assault occurs when an individual is placed in a position where he is in reasonable fear of non-consensual touching which is harmful or offensive to him. If a person is hit over the head with a club, the assault is seeing the club directed at him and fearing that he will be hit, while the battery is actually being hit by the club. If the same person were hit over the head while sleeping, the claim of battery would still prevail, but the assault claim would lack the critical element of fear or apprehension.

Most cases of assault and battery in the medical malpractice context occur because a practitioner undertakes to perform a procedure without securing the necessary informed consent. See Chapter 4. A medical procedure performed most skillfully will still amount to a battery if the patient did not agree to it or would not have agreed had he been adequately informed about it. Alternatively, in some cases battery is alleged notwithstanding the patient's consent to treatment if the treatment goes beyond the scope of the consent. In *Schloendorff v. Society of New York Hospital* (N.Y.1914), a patient who allegedly consented to examination under ether brought an action in intentional tort against the physician because the physician performed a subsequent operation for which there had been no prior agreement. More recently, in *Perna v. Pirozzi* (N.J. 1983), a patient brought suit in intentional tort because she had consented to an operation to be performed by one surgeon and it was thereafter performed by another physician. The vast majority of assault and battery cases brought against medical practitioners occur in the context of inadequate consent.

Sometimes cases are brought in intentional tort against medical personnel who employ measures intended to restrain patients for medical treatment. Psychiatric personnel, for example, sometimes need to use physical force to restrain a patient, and thereafter may be sued for undue force. These cases are generally decided upon the facts of the individual case as to whether the nature of the force was reasonable and warranted under the circumstances. A variation on that theme occurred in *Mattocks v. Bell* (D.C.App.1963). In this case, a two year old child was being treated by a medical student for a lacerated tongue. During the procedure the child bit down on the student's finger and would not release it. After several unsuccessful efforts to free his finger, the student struck the child on the cheek. In a subsequent action for intentional tort, the court held that the amount of force was proper under the circumstances, therefore negating any liability.

B. SEXUAL EXPLOITATION

An increasingly large number of plaintiffs have brought malpractice actions against practitioners, notably mental health professionals, for battery as a consequence of engaging the plaintiffs in sexual activity during, after, or as a part of, treatment. It is consistently held, particularly in the context of mental health treatment, that it is completely improper and unethical for a practitioner to suggest, agree or in any other way participate in a sexual relationship with a current patient. Often, it is considered improper to engage in sexual relations with former patients as well. Some states impose criminal penalties for such conduct and virtually all states recognize it to be the basis for a civil action. See Fla. Stat. § 491.0112 (2002). Many states impose civil monetary penalties for such conduct. See 740 ILCS 140/2 (2003). Depending upon the facts of a case, improper sexual relations with patients may result in either negligence or intentional tort claims.

In *Simmons v. United States* (9th Cir.1986), the court explained the theory under which cases of sexual exploitation are deemed to constitute negligence. In short, psychiatric patients often develop an attachment to, and a dependence upon, the doctor as an intended consequence of the treatment. Known as transference reactions, therapy patients routinely develop strong feelings toward the therapist that make them vulnerable to abuse by an unethical therapist who exploits the power and position that arises by virtue of the transference process. Thus in *Simmons,* the court held that the therapist's sexual abuse of the patient constituted a mishandling of the transference reaction and, therefore, professional negligence. Even though the standard defense to exploitation is consent of the patient, the literature and the cases clearly indicate that the consent of such a patient is invalid because of the involuntary transference reaction and the coercive nature of the relationship.

In *Benavidez v. United States,* a federal district court distinguished intentional tort claims from those based in negligence. The court reasoned that an intentional tort of assault and battery arose where the defendant "intentionally misused his therapeutic relationship with the plaintiff to force the plaintiff to engage in sexual contact with him." Benavidez v. United States (D.N.M. 1997). The 10th Circuit reversed, however, holding that consent is essentially irrelevant in the therapeutic context and such conduct has traditionally been defined in terms of negligence.

In earlier cases alleging sexual exploitation, plaintiffs were faced with the dilemma of whether to plead their case in intentional tort (assault and battery, criminal conversation, alienation of affections) which seemed to best define the wrong and did not require the court to understand the transference principles to establish negligence. The problem with pleading in intentional tort was that professional liability carriers would generally disclaim coverage for those acts which did not seemingly arise out of the professional treatment. The alternative, of course, was to allege that the sexual activity did arise out of treatment, and to attempt to prove that it resulted from the malpractice of the practitioner.

Much of the dilemma has been eliminated by two recent changes. First, today a growing number of courts now recognize the true nature of the exploitation claim, thus eliminating the barriers for plaintiffs to establish that they were wrongfully treated.

In fact, the existence of civil and criminal penalties in some states demonstrates that exploitation is certainly not a consensual undertaking. Secondly, today, professional liability carriers routinely disclaim insurance coverage for sexual exploitation, regardless of how the matter is pleaded, so that the dilemma of how to present the case is no longer significant.

C.   DEFAMATION

Defamation refers to the wrongful injury to reputation that is caused by communicating a false statement either orally (as in slander) or in writing (as in libel). In the context of medical practitioners, defamation can occur when a patient is wrongfully reported to have a certain disease (e.g., Acquired Immune Deficiency Syndrome (AIDS)), carry a contagious condition (e.g., tuberculosis) or display a certain psychological or character flaw (e.g., paranoia). It is critical in proving a case of defamation that the communication be "published" (i.e., communicated to a third party) by the defendant accused of defamation.

A medical practitioner alleged to have defamed another is not without defense. The most clear-cut defense is that the statement, although it may have caused injury, was nevertheless true. Truth is generally an absolute defense to defamation. However, another intentional tort, such as invasion of privacy, may occur if the information revealed was privileged. Other defenses used to defeat a defamation claim include: (1) privilege to communicate, such as when ordered for purposes of a judicial proceeding; (2) formal or informal statements made about patients to other physicians for purposes of discussing treatment. False statements made by a practitioner under the above circumstances are privileged are privileged and do not amount to defamation.

Courts differ on the question of whether the defendant has to be negligent (or more, such as reckless) in communicating information which turns out to be false or whether an honest mistake in the knowledge about the truth of the matter will support a claim of defamation. What is clear is that in the context of public figures or public officials, the defendant must either have actual knowledge or reckless disregard for the truth or falsity of the statement in order to be held accountable for defamation.

Sometimes statements are made that would otherwise be defamatory but are protected by a privilege or a qualified privilege in order to protect an important medical interest. For example, in *Simonsen v. Swenson* (Neb.1920), a physician received the results of a preliminary test which indicated that his patient had syphilis. Fearing that he might be contagious, the physician communicated the information to certain persons. It was eventually determined that the patient did not, in fact, have the disease, and that the physician's communication caused him harm. In the subsequent suit for defamation, however, the court declined to impose liability on the physician, holding that he had a duty to disclose the preliminary information and thus was protected in doing so.

D. FALSE IMPRISONMENT

False imprisonment is a tort which results when a person is intentionally detained in an unlawful manner or otherwise restricted in movement without privilege or consent of the individual. Among the more common examples in the medical context are patients who are not released from the hospital because of failure to pay a bill or failure to sign various forms for billing of third party payors. Another common example is the psychiatric patient or non-psychiatric patient who demonstrates emotional problems and is wrongfully confined without justifiable cause. A patient who has not been lawfully committed to an appropriate facility has no obligation to stay, and physical or coercive efforts to restrict movement may constitute false imprisonment. In *Marcus v. Liebman* (Ill.App.1978), a patient who voluntarily admitted herself to a psychiatric unit of a general hospital eventually wanted to leave. The physician coerced her into staying at the hospital by threatening to commit her to a state institution if she left. The court determined that plaintiff was entitled to have a jury decide whether the patient had be falsely imprisoned.

A closely related cause of action that sometimes occurs in the context of involuntary commitment is abuse of process. This may occur when a physician, without justifiable cause, participates in a judicial proceeding to involuntarily commit or continue the commitment of an individual in a psychiatric facility. In *Maniaci v. Marquette University* (Wis.1971), a college freshman who was discovered leaving campus was stopped by university officials. In order to detain her, they initiated commitment proceedings to a hospital. In her subsequent lawsuit, the Wisconsin Supreme Court ultimately found that while an action for false imprisonment would not lie because the university had complied with legal procedures for involuntary commitment, there may have been a viable claim for abuse of process.

E. INVASION OF PRIVACY

Invasion of privacy claims are generally limited to conduct that would be highly offensive to the ordinary person. Invasion of privacy occurs in the medical context when the legitimate privacy interests of patients are publicized to another person, whether or not the publicity casts the patient in some sort of derogatory light. Sometimes privacy interests are invaded by wrongful disclosure of confidential information, which will be discussed in the next section. Pure privacy claims, however, might be triggered by using, without permission, pictures that are taken of a patient during medical treatment or to demonstrate a particular result. In *Vassiliades v. Garfinckel's, Brooks Bros.* (D.C.App. 1985), the defendant allegedly used "before" and "after" photographs of a patient's cosmetic surgery without obtaining her consent for their use. The plaintiff prevailed on theories of both invasion of privacy and breach of fiduciary obligation on the basis that she had suffered unwanted publicity in connection with the photographs.

The fact that information revealed is truthful is not a defense to an invasion of privacy claim. By the same token, privilege is not generally successful in defending a claim. If, for example, a patient's case history is used for textbook or instructional purposes (rather than informal consultation) the patient is entitled to confidentiality. The name should not be revealed, nor should any readily identifying information that would cause the patient's identity to be known. The new HIPAA privacy rules specifically address this type of patient privacy. See 104 P.L. 191 § 264 (1996); 45 C.F.R. Part 164 (2000).

Physicians have sometimes been held liable for revealing private information about patients that is not necessarily expressly privileged nor disclosed as a consequence of the physician-patient relationship. For example, if a patient, while hospitalized, reveals to a physician a story about something that happened to her which is not pertinent to her treatment, but merely a personal tale, and the physician repeats it to a third party, a theory of liability might be fashioned against the physician for invasion of privacy, even if the communication was not related to treatment.

F. MISREPRESENTATION

A physician who negligently or intentionally misstates or conceals an important fact concerning a patient for the purpose of influencing treatment decisions or concealing treatment results may be liable for misrepresentation. Misrepresentation is closely related to another intentional tort, fraud, which may occur when a physician intentionally conceals an important fact concerning treatment that might affect the outcome, or the actions of the patient following treatment. If, for example, a physician performs a procedure negligently and then conceals his negligence by misrepresenting the error to the patient, this may constitute both fraud and misrepresentation, and a subsequent action may lie for both claims.

In order to recover for the tort of misrepresentation, it is necessary to establish that the person to whom the misrepresentation was made relied upon it. In *Simcuski v. Saeli* (N.Y.1978), the plaintiff claimed misrepresentation upon evidence that the defendant physician, knowing that the patient suffered post-operative problems as a result of the negligent manner in which he performed surgery, nevertheless allowed her to think that the complications were transient and concealed the fact that there was treatment available.

G. DISCLOSURE OF CONFIDENTIAL INFORMATION

A physician who, without consent or other cause, discloses to another confidential information about a patient which was learned within the physician-patient relationship, may be liable for breach of confidentiality. See *Horne v. Patton* (Ala.1973); *MacDonald v. Clinger* (N.Y.A.D.1982). The duty to maintain confidentiality was originally derived from the Hippocratic Oath. In addition, several state and federal statutes, including the new HIPPA privacy rules and state licensing statutes, protect the confidentiality of medical information. See, e.g., Drug Abuse and Treatment Acts and Alcohol Prevention, Treatment and Rehabilitation Act, 42 U.S.C.A. §§ 290dd–3, 390ee–3.

The reasons for confidentiality in the physician-patient relationship are straightforward. Medical treatment is often a private matter, during which patients discuss private and confidential issues with their physicians. In order to obtain the best possible care, patients need to freely and openly discuss all matters that relate to their care and treatment. Some matters may be highly sensitive or even embarrassing, while others may harm the patient if revealed. The ability of the patient to speak candidly requires that confidentiality be maintained. Statutes regulating licensing and testimonial privileges have sometimes been cited for the proposition that a cause of action exists for breach of confidentiality. See *Biddle v. Warren General Hosp.* (Ohio 1999)(Holding that absent prior authorization, a physician or hospital is privileged to disclose otherwise confidential medical information in those special situations where disclosure is made in accordance with a statutory mandate or common-law duty, or where disclosure is necessary to protect or further a countervailing interest which outweighs the patient's interest in confidentiality). Statutes concerning testimonial privileges generally hold that disclosure of confidential information is prohibited, even in the context of a judicial proceeding, unless the court first determines in the interest of justice that the privilege is waived.

In those cases in which a patient seeks the services of a physician for reasons other than medical treatment, the confidentiality of the relationship is qualified. Thus if a patient, who makes a claim under a workers' compensation statute, is sent to the adverse party's physician to determine if the claim is warranted, the result of the examination is probably not privileged, at least as to the adverse party. Similarly, if an employer or a life insurance company sends an applicant for a medical examination, the results of the examination will not be privileged as to the party requiring the patient to undergo the exam. See *Millsaps v. Bankers Life Co.* (Ill.App.1976).

By the same token, a plaintiff who places her medical condition into issue by virtue of filing a lawsuit and claiming damages impliedly waives the testimonial privilege that would prevent a physician from testifying in the matter. See *Bond v. District Court* (Colo.1984) (seeking reversal of a discovery order pertaining to the treatment notes of a therapist where patient had put her mental pain and suffering into issue). Furthermore, physicians routinely consult one another to discuss patient care, exchange information, and discuss treatment plans. *Supra* Chapter 3, Section B. It is important to watch judicial interpretation of the new HIPAA privacy rules which go into effect as this book goes to press. Prior to this federal legislation, the general rule was that no liability would arise even though the identity of the patient is disclosed.

In some cases, a patient's spouse is entitled (by statute or case law) to certain information about a patient, particularly under circumstances that it is necessary to protect the spouse. Similarly, sometimes parents or other family members are entitled to access certain information. By the same token, if a patient presents a danger of imminent threat to a third person, a physician may have an obligation to protect the third person, either by confining the dangerous person or warning the target of his aggressions. See *Tarasoff v. Regents of the University of California* (Cal.1976) and its progeny, supra at Chapter 2.

Under some circumstances, a physician is required to disclose otherwise confidential information by virtue of statutory mandatory reporting requirements. In cases of child abuse, gunshot wounds, contagious diseases and certain other matters, physicians are both obligated to report such findings and immunized from liability for disclosure of related confidential information. Nevertheless, the disclosure is limited to the information required to carry out the intent of the reporting requirements, and should not be abused. Physicians should be careful not to disclose peripheral information in the context of a mandated report. Notwithstanding statutory immunity, some courts have held that because the privilege of disclosure is conditional, it is abused if the information is either intentionally false or communicated with reckless disregard for its truth. The privilege is preserved if the disclosure is made in good faith, even though the information turns out to be false. Most courts will also maintain the privilege for mere negligence in disclosure.

II. EMOTIONAL DISTRESS AND OUTRAGE

When a medical practitioner acts in such a manner that is extreme and outrageous, and in so doing causes emotional distress, an independent tort may be triggered. Infliction of emotional distress may be alleged as either an intentional or negligent act. It is not easy to determine whether a jury will conclude that the infliction of emotional distress was intentional or negligent, though the distinction may be critical to the outcome of the case. In general, conduct that is extreme and outrageous or reckless is intentional while less culpable conduct that also causes emotional distress may be negligent.

Often the characterization as "negligent" or "intentional" is critical because of statutory or procedural implications. As previously mentioned, often insurance liability coverage may be jeopardized in cases of intentional wrongdoing. If so, the characterization may affect the availability of coverage. Furthermore, many courts hold that in order to claim damages for conduct was negligent, it must have produced some sort of physical manifestation (post-traumatic stress disorder, cardiac arrest, etc.). If, however, the conduct was extreme and outrageous, the requirement of physical manifestation might be eliminated.

In those cases in which the person claiming emotional distress is not the patient but instead a "bystander" who witnesses the injury of another, courts typically hold that the "test" for recovery of damages for emotional distress is whether the distress to the bystander was "foreseeable" as a consequence of the alleged conduct. In *Thing v. La Chusa* (Cal.1989), the court held that "foreseeability" was a function of whether the plaintiff (1) was closely related to the injury victim; (2) was present at the scene of the injury and aware of the harm; and (3) as a result suffered the type of severe emotional harm that would be normally anticipated as a consequences of the circumstances.

The "foreseeability" approach was used in *Johnson v. Ruark Obstetrics and Gynecology Associates, P.A.* (N.C.1990), where expectant parents of a stillborn fetus alleged that they observed the events that led to the death of their fetus. On a motion to dismiss, the court allowed the claim of negligent infliction of emotional distress to go forward on grounds of reasonable foreseeability. This approach is often used for claims of emotional distress by bystanders who witness injury to a loved one and would be expected to suffer harm as a result.

A number of courts have articulated the need for the bystander to be within a "zone of danger" in order to recover for emotional distress. In *Whetham v. Bismarck Hosp.* (N.D.1972), a mother who allegedly observed her newborn infant being dropped was considered to be within the zone of danger and thus able to fear that his safety was in jeopardy. Other courts, however, reject the zone of danger requirement, holding that recovery would be permitted if the bystander was present, observed the injury, was closely related to the patient and suffered emotional consequences as a result. On the other hand, in at least one case, a bystander was denied recovery because he was a "voluntary" witness to the occurrence. Thus in *Justus v. Atchison* (Cal.1977), a father who chose to be present in the delivery room was denied recovery as a bystander when complications arose that allegedly resulted in the death of his child. Having voluntarily undertaken to observe in the delivery room, he no longer qualified as a bystander who happened to witness an injury. The broad holding in *Justus* was qualified, however, in *Ochoa v. Superior Court* (Cal. 1985). The court determined that the voluntary or involuntary presence of the plaintiff should not be the decisive factor in determining whether the plaintiff may recover.

Other courts reject the "zone of danger" requirement by permitting recovery only if a bystander was present, observed the injury, was closely related to the victim, and suffered emotional consequences as a result. *See* City of Austin v. Davis (Tex.App.1985). The U.S. Supreme Court, however, adopted a narrow interpretation of the common law "zone of danger" test. *See* Consolidated Rail Corporation v. Gottshall (S.Ct.1994) (adopting standard for evaluating negligent infliction of emotional distress under Federal Employers' Liability Act (FELA)). This test limits liability to those victims sustaining physical injury as a result of the defendant's negligent conduct or those placed in the immediate risk of physical harm by the conduct. *See id.* at 546.

In at least one case, a bystander was denied recovery because he was deemed to be a "voluntary" witness to the occurrence. In *Justus v. Atchison* (Cal.1977), a father witnessed the death of his child arising from complications experienced in the delivery room. The court held that the father did not qualify as a bystander because he asked to observe the birth of his child. The broad holding in Justus, however, was qualified in *Ochoa v. Superior Court* (Cal. 1985). The court determined that the voluntary or involuntary presence of the plaintiff should not be the decisive factor in determining whether the plaintiff should recover.

If a contractual relationship exists between the parties and it becomes the basis for the emotional distress claim, some courts relax the standard by eliminating the presence requirement. In *Newton v. Kaiser Hospital* (Cal.App.1986), the parents of a handicapped newborn alleged that the child was born partially handicapped because the physician failed to deliver the child by caesarean section. Neither parent actually observed the delivery as the mother was unconscious and the father was not present. The court held that the physician's contractual obligation to deliver a healthy baby established his duty, and did not require proximity or witnessing by the parents.

Yet another line of cases in which a contractual relationship forms the basis for a claim of emotional distress is exemplified by *Mazza v. Huffaker* (N.C.App.1983). In that case, a psychiatrist who treated a patient for four years thereafter developed an intimate (sexual) relationship with the patient's wife. The standard of care for psychiatrists at that time strictly forbid such a relationship on the basis of the harm that it would cause to the patient. The psychiatrist was found liable both in malpractice and infliction of emotional distress on the basis of the contractual duty owed to the patient. See also *Rowe v. Bennett* (Me.1986), for the same holding under a similar set of circumstances.

The more difficult cases allegedly causing emotional distress are those in which a practitioner's neglect or unprofessional conduct causes harm to the patient. In these cases the harm is generally not caused by medical practice or malpractice, and often the claim is defended on that basis. Usually courts will find a basis for allowing such claims, however, often labeling them torts of "outrage" or similar terms. For example, in *Johnson v. Woman's Hospital* (Tenn.App.1975), a woman who had lost a child during a premature birth sought information regarding the disposition of the child's body. After encountering much difficulty in ascertaining what had happened to the child's body, the mother was eventually directed to a hospital employee who presented to her a jar of formaldehyde containing the body of the infant. The court held that such action would clearly sustain the mother's claim of outrage.

In *Chew v. Paul D. Meyer, M.D., P.A.* (Md.App. 1987), the plaintiff presented to his physician an employment claim form to document his absence from work. He specifically told the physician that it had to be completed and returned to his employer promptly, or he could lose his job. Despite repeated inquiries, however, eighteen days elapsed before the form was returned, and the plaintiff lost his job as a result. The court allowed the plaintiff's action to go forward on the basis that the defendant had undertaken a contractual duty to the patient, and that his failure to perform resulted in damages to the plaintiff. Thus although the underlying claim was not one of medical negligence, the claim of mental distress was nevertheless supported.

There have been some cases in which the medical practitioner's unprofessional conduct served as the basis for the claim of emotional distress. In *Anderson v. Prease* (D.C.App.1982), the defendant was alleged to have screamed and cursed at the plaintiff, insisting that she leave his office. Finding that a viable claim existed, the court noted that the physician apparently knew that the plaintiff had a nervous condition that could make her particularly vulnerable to emotional distress as a consequence of those actions.

Patients exposed to contaminated blood during treatment have sued for negligent infliction of emotional distress based on the fear of acquiring the HIV virus. In *K.A.C. v. Benson* (Minn.1995), a plaintiff sued a physician with AIDS for performing gynecological examinations on her with open sores on his hands. The court dismissed her claim, holding that the plaintiff was not in the zone of danger because she failed to establish actual exposure to HIV. The majority of courts hold that a plaintiff must allege actual exposure to HIV to establish a claim of negligent infliction of emotional distress. A minority of courts, however, do not require actual exposure. *See Faya v. Almaraz* (Md.1993).

III. VIOLATION OF CIVIL RIGHTS

There have been numerous contexts in which medical malpractice plaintiffs have alleged that their civil rights have been violated. Both the federal Civil Rights Act and its state counterparts have been invoked to cover medical practices and physician's services. In some cases, plaintiffs have alleged discrimination in their access to services on the basis of race or national origin. In other cases, plaintiffs have cited specific statutory authority which has been developed to assist patients in exercising their civil rights. For example, in *Reid v. Indianapolis Osteopathic Medical Hosp., Inc.* (S.D.Ind.1989), the plaintiff brought an action under 42 U.S.C.A. § 1395dd, which is a federal statute designed to deter hospitals from "dumping" patients in need of medical care because of the patients' inability to pay. The statute seems to give such plaintiffs a private right of action and to recover damages in accordance with the malpractice laws of the state in which the hospital is located. See Chapter 8.

In *Leach v. Drummond Medical Group,* supra at chapter 1, patients who were part of a medical group were denied services because they filed a complaint with the medical licensing board against the group of physicians serving them. In their subsequent suit to compel the medical group to provide treatment, the court held that the plaintiffs had stated a cause of action under the state's Civil Rights Act, and that the physicians' refusal to treat the patients constituted arbitrary discrimination in violation of the statute. A complete analysis of the civil rights acts and related legislation and their applicability to potential claims of malpractice plaintiffs is beyond the scope of this book.

Yet another line of cases that have alleged "intentional" violation of civil rights are those involving the involuntary commitment of psychiatric patients, as well as the forcible administration of anti-psychotic medication in order to manage such patients once they are committed. Specific statutory guidelines exist for involuntary commitment, and failure to adhere to such guidelines has been held to infringe on the civil rights of those affected. Both federal and state civil rights acts have been invoked in order to enjoin the commitment and/or establish a private right of action for damages. See, e.g., *Widgeon v. Eastern Shore Hospital Center* (Md. 1984).

Finally, there is a growing number of cases brought primarily against mental health professionals who become sexually involved with their patients. A number of cases have been brought, typically under either a specific statute or under a malpractice theory. See *Simmons v. United States*, supra; *Mazza v. Huffaker*, supra. To the extent that a civil rights act is held to cover medical practices, a cause of action may also exist for sexual exploitation as a violation of civil rights.

Testing a patient for HIV without consent has been held to be a violation of the equal protection clause of the United States Constitution. Hill v. Evans (M.D.Ala.1993). Most states require specific consent in order to test a patient for HIV or AIDS. *See* Identification and Management of Asymptomatic HIV–Infected Persons in New Jersey (3d ed. 1996) § 1.3; N.Y. Pub. Health Law § 2781(c) (McKinney 1993 & Supp. 1998); Conn. Gen. Stat. Ann. § 19a–582(b)(4) (West 1993). Mass. Gen. Law c. 111 § 70F.

CHAPTER FOUR

INFORMED DECISION MAKING

I. IN GENERAL: BATTERY vs. NEGLIGENCE

The modern doctrine of informed consent is a logical outgrowth of the common law concept of battery, which is defined as an unlawful, non-consensual touching. Battery theory has been used in the health care law field to impose liability on a health care provider who performs a procedure without first obtaining the informed consent of his or her patient. Over time, negligence theory has replaced common law battery as the basis for litigation. Most of the modern cases involving informed consent address the question of whether or not the physician provided sufficient information to the patient; these cases focus on the quantity and quality of that information. It is unusual, but not impossible, for a case to arise today in which no consent at all was given. Since procedures performed by physicians or other health care providers usually involve a touching of a patient's body, the law protects the right of a person not to be touched without consent and authorization. This concept is well rooted in common law as well as American constitutional law. The right of self-determination was articulated by

Justice Cardozo in his opinion in the case of *Schloendorff v. Society of New York Hospital* (N.Y. 1914):

> Every human being of adult years and sound mind has a right to determine what shall be done with his own body, and a surgeon who performs an operation without his patient's consent commits an assault for which he is liable in damages.

This concept is central to the constitutional right to privacy. See *Griswold v. Connecticut* (S.Ct.1965); *Roe v. Wade* (S.Ct.1973), *Hondroulis v. Schuhmacher* (La.1988).

There are two types of cases involving informed consent. The first type, and the one that is seen in most courts today, is the negligence case. In a negligence case, the question is whether the patient, prior to giving consent, received that amount and type of information that a reasonable person would require in order to make an informed decision as to whether to undergo the medical procedure. In the second type of case, assault and battery, the issue before the court is whether consent was given at all.

A negligence action alleging failure to obtain informed consent is the more common claim. Negligence arises when a physician fails to communicate sufficient material information about the proposed procedure for the patient to make an informed decision. In *Lugenbuhl v. Dowling* (La.1997), a doctor failed to disclose his intention not to use mesh to close a wound, as promised to the patient, in the event the operative conditions differed from what was expected in a hernia procedure. The court reasoned that the patient was unable to fully consent to the procedure because the doctor failed to disclose material information.

The assault and battery cases may involve one or more of the following: (1) no consent was obtained; (2) a procedure completely or substantially different from the one authorized was performed; or (3) the procedure exceeded the scope of consent obtained. In *Blanchard v. Kellum*, (Tenn.1998), the plaintiff successfully brought a battery claim after her dentist extracted all thirty-two of her teeth in a single office visit. The patient had not been fully informed on the extent of the procedure before it was performed.

Although the theories of battery and negligence may appear similar in many respects, there are differences which may have a dramatic effect on the pending action. One such difference is the statute of limitations. In some jurisdictions, the statute of limitations for battery cases is different from that of negligence cases. Other jurisdictions have enacted statutes applying to all actions against health care providers, in effect making the statute of limitations the same whether the action is filed under a battery or negligence theory. (See Massachusetts General Laws, ch. 260, § 4.)

Another difference between the battery theory and the negligence theory relates to damages. In a negligence action, the successful plaintiff is entitled to recover compensatory damages resulting from the physician's failure to disclose certain risks which materialized. In a battery action, the successful plaintiff may recover for the unlawful touching, for all injuries resulting from the unlawful touching and, in some cases, punitive damages.

II. PATIENT'S RIGHT TO INFORMATION

In order for a physician to lawfully perform a medical procedure on a patient, the patient must consent to the treatment. The most common manifestation of consent is when the patient, after receiving the necessary information, specifically requests that the procedure be performed. See Restatement (Second) of Torts § 892A and comment b. (1979)

A. CONSENT: A BASIC REQUIREMENT

There are many ways in which the patient can express his consent to the treating physician. Written or oral manifestations are both acceptable. The limits of express consent and authorization by the patient should be clear and easy to identify. A written consent form is the usual procedure for obtaining a patient's express consent and may even be required in some jurisdictions. See West's Fla. Stat. Ann. § 766.103 (1988); Ohio Stat. § 2317.54 (Baldwin 2002). See *Hondroulis v. Schumacher* (La. 1988). (Signed consent form tracking state statute established a rebuttable presumption of consent).

A good consent form should include at least the following provisions:

1.   Patient's name.

2.   Date and time of consent.

3.   Patient's condition or problem, preferably in nontechnical language.

4.   Nature and purpose of the proposed procedure, preferably in non-technical language.

5.   Name of the physician who explained the proposed procedure and is obtaining consent.

6.   All material risks of the proposed procedure.

7.   Treatment alternatives, including non-treatment.

8.   Prognosis and risks of treatment alternatives, including non-treatment.

9.   Disclaimer of any warranty or guarantee of success.

10.   Identification of the physician who will perform the procedure, if different from the physician obtaining consent.

11.   Consent of the patient to the procedure.

12.   Consent of the patient to allow the physician to deviate or modify the procedure if unforeseen circumstances arise during the course of the procedure. Any limitations should be noted.

13.   Acknowledgment that the patient has been given the opportunity to ask questions and that any such questions have been answered.

14. Consent of the patient to disposal of removed organs and tissue if applicable.

15. Signature of patient or legal guardian (if the patient is a child or incompetent) and a witness.

Unless the doctor and patient are in a jurisdiction where written consent is required, unwritten or oral consent may also be valid. This has its roots in an old Massachusetts case, *O'Brien v. Cunard S.S. Co.* (Mass.1891). The Supreme Judicial Court of Massachusetts held that the plaintiff consented to vaccination by standing in a line and holding out her arm to a doctor who was vaccinating passengers on a ship. The court stated that silence implies consent if the circumstances are such that a reasonable person would speak if the person had an objection. Although oral consent may be upheld as valid, in terms of clear proof, a writing is preferred.

There are other ways that the patient may consent without overtly manifesting her willingness to the doctor. In some cases the patient may actually be an unwilling participant in the treatment, but the requirements of proper informed consent are nevertheless fulfilled. *Infra* Ch.4, Section C. For example, if an unconscious patient presents in an Emergency Room with a life-threatening condition, the principles of implied consent would be invoked so that treatment could proceed. Implied consent is a legal fiction established to enable emergency medical personnel to initiate emergency treatment without delay. Consent is "implied" by the circumstances and actual consent is not required. See section (C) below.

If a patient exhibits certain conduct that would indicate that he or she is willing to undergo a medical procedure, regardless of the patient's state of mind or tacit unwillingness to undergo the treatment, the patient can be deemed to have consented to the treatment. Restatement (Second) of Torts § 892 and comment c. This is only true if the doctor reasonably understands that the patient's conduct signifies consent. The doctor also must act in good faith in concluding that the patient's conduct accurately reflects a willingness by the patient to undergo the medical treatment.

Traditionally, courts have deemed minors incompetent to give consent to medical treatment unless they are "emancipated." In such cases, consent of a parent or guardian generally must be obtained before procedures are performed on the minor. See *Zoski v. Gaines* (Mich.1935). Of course, during an emergency situation when the child's life is at stake, or serious bodily harm may occur, the doctor may perform a procedure on the patient without parental consent. Some jurisdictions have statutes which grant immunity for physicians, dentists and hospitals which do not obtain the consent of a parent, legal guardian or other person having custody of a minor child when emergency treatment is necessary. See Mass. Gen. Laws Ch. 112, § 12F.

In some jurisdictions, a mature minor may be deemed capable of giving informed consent. An example is a case in which a minor presents for treatment requesting a procedure that is simple and beneficial and time is of the essence (although it is not an emergency). If the child's parents cannot be reached, the doctor may proceed on the minor's consent, if the minor is deemed mature enough to make such a decision. See *Younts v. St. Francis Hosp. and School of Nursing, Inc.* (Kan.1970). But see *Belcher v. Charleston Area Medical Ctr.* (W.Va. 1992) (holding that even if the patient is a "mature minor" both the minor's consent and the parent's consent are required).

"Emancipated" minors, or minors who have left their parents' control by marrying, entering military service or by other means, are, in some jurisdictions, given the right to give consent to medical or dental treatment without parental consent. See Mass. Gen. Laws Ch. 112, § 12F.

During the past thirty years, many courts, including the Supreme Court of the United States, have allowed minors faced with what traditionally have been termed "adult issues" to consent to treatment without parental consent. Examples of these situations include treatment of alcohol or drug addictions, treatment of sexually transmitted diseases and treatment following rape, prescription of birth control pills, and treatment concerning the minor's own child. *Cardwell v. Bechtol* (Tenn.1987).

The right to an abortion, including the right of minors to seek an abortion has been debated since the seminal decision of *Roe v. Wade* (S.Ct.1973).

The issue of whether parental consent is necessary for a minor child to seek an abortion was raised three years later in the case of *Planned Parenthood of Central Mo. v. Danforth* (S.Ct.1976). In *Danforth*, the Supreme Court found Missouri's statute to be unconstitutional in that it required all minors to obtain parental consent before having an abortion. The issue still lingers. In 1979 the Supreme Court upheld a parental consent requirement, so long as there existed an alternative procedure allowing the minor to seek authorization through the judicial process. See *Bellotti v. Baird* (S.Ct.1979) (requiring a judicial by-pass mechanism); *H.L. v. Matheson* (S.Ct.1981) (parental notice permitted under Utah law, but parents have no veto power.)

B. SCOPE OF CONSENT

A patient may consent to a procedure, but the issues regarding the extent or scope of the patient's consent still remain. Traditionally, physicians may not expand the procedure beyond the scope of a patient's consent even when the expanded treatment is related to the consented procedure. See *Mohr v. Williams* (Minn.1905) and *Perry v. Hodgson* (Ga.1929). However, there are exceptions. When a physician, during the course of an operation, thinks that further action must be taken without delay in order to preserve the patient's life or save her from serious harm, then the scope may be expanded. See *Preston v. Hubbell* (Cal.App.1948).

Courts also have allowed a physician to use his or her reasonable judgment in deciding whether to expand the scope of a medical procedure. The so-called "extension doctrine" may apply if unforeseen problems arise while the physician is performing a procedure and additional treatment is thus required. If failure to address those problems would compromise the well-being of the patient, and the patient is unable to give an informed consent, the doctor may be entitled to "extend" the scope of the original consent in order to address the problem. Some courts have limited this "extension" to use in emergency situations. See *Danielson v. Roche* (Cal. App.1952); *Rothe v. Hull* (Mo.1944). In *Mohr*, supra, that court held a doctor's decision to perform a procedure on the patient's left ear was actionable where the patient's consent was only for the right ear; even though the court found that the condition was serious, it was not an emergency. Contra, *Buzzell v. Libi* (N.D.1983).

The extension doctrine was applied in a 1956 North Carolina case to absolve from liability a physician who performed an additional procedure. *Kennedy v. Parrott* (N.C.1956). The physician, during the course of an appendectomy, discovered and punctured some ovarian cysts which he found, without first obtaining the patient's informed consent. The Supreme Court of North Carolina held that the patient could not give consent, the condition could not have been diagnosed prior to treatment, there was no indication that the patient would not consent to the procedure, the extension was in the area of the original incision, and there was sound medical justification for extending the authorized surgery. Accordingly, the physician incurred no liability.

Finally, in some jurisdictions courts have held, under the extension doctrine, that a care-giver may expand the scope of the patient's consent in a wider range of situations. Based on the notion that "no reasonable person would object if in a position to make a decision" a practitioner can act if he reasonably believes that an extension of the original procedure is in the best interest of the patient. See W. Keeton. D. Dobbs, R. Keeton & D. Owen, Prosser & Keeton on the Law of Torts § 18: at 117–8 (5th ed. 1984).

C. IMPLIED OR SUBSTITUTED CONSENT

If a person is brought into a hospital or doctor's office unconscious, with injuries that appear to be life-threatening, medical personnel may provide that person with treatment, even though that person is unable to consent. The concept that allows the provider to act without express consent is the legal fiction known as "implied consent." The theory behind implied consent is that it is in the public interest to have medical personnel provide care to critically ill patients or patients with life-threatening conditions without fear of legal action. See *Hernandez v. United States* (D.Kan.1979); *Jackovach v. Yocom* (Iowa 1931). Implied consent has been held to exist even in non-emergent situations. See *O'Brien v. Cunard S.S. Co., Ltd.* (Mass.1891). (Holding out one's arm, consent to vaccination).

When a person cannot, or is not competent to, give consent to medical treatment, the law sometimes allows for the patient's relatives or guardian to give consent for the patient. This theory is known as substituted consent. See *In re Estate of Longeway* (Ill.1989); and *In re Estate of Greenspan* (Ill.1990).

Much of the case law surrounding substituted consent arises out of the parent-and-child relationship. In many jurisdictions, minors are considered incapable of consenting to treatment and the surrogate decision-maker will more often than not be a parent or guardian. Generally, it is appropriate for the parent to make a medical choice for a child who cannot consent; however, that parent also must possess the mental capacity to give or withhold consent to treatment.

Recently, courts have held that a parent may not force a child to undergo a medical procedure, if it is not in the best interest of the child or is against the wishes of the other parent. In the case of *Curran v. Bosze* (Ill.1990), the father of three and one-half year-old twins sought an order compelling the twins to submit to bone marrow harvesting so that they could donate bone marrow to their half brother who suffered from leukemia. This was against the wishes of the twins' mother. The court ruled in favor of the mother and held that (1) the doctrine of substituted consent did not apply and (2) the bone marrow harvesting was not in the best interests of the twins.

Substituted consent should be distinguished from the doctrine of substituted judgment, which is used quite frequently with regard to patients who are comatose or otherwise unable to communicate. Substituted judgment authorizes a surrogate decision-maker to make treatment decisions on behalf of an individual who lacks capacity to do so. The surrogate must "establish, with as much accuracy as possible, what decision the patient would make if [the patient] were competent to do so." *Longeway*, supra.

The role of the surrogate decision-maker has changed in recent years with the passage of statutes allowing a "living will" or a "health care proxy." These statutes allow patients to document in advance their wishes in a living will or in a health care proxy. Patients can articulate through these documents when and if they would like to withhold or withdraw life-sustaining procedures, or to designate someone to make decisions for them. In the absence of one of these "advance directives", the surrogate decision-maker must "determine with as much accuracy as possible, the wants and needs of the person involved." See *Brophy v. New England Sinai Hospital* (Mass.1986).

Generally, if a situation is not life-threatening, a patient may refuse treatment if he or she is competent to do so. *Riggins v. Nevada* (S.Ct.1992) (It was error to order that a person charged with murder be administered anti-psychotic drugs during his murder trial over his objection). If the patient's condition is life-threatening and any doubt remains regarding the patient's competency, courts are reluctant to allow patients the option to refuse "nonheroic" life-saving measures. See *Matter of Storar* (N.Y.1981); see also *Westchester County Med. Ctr.* (N.Y.1988).

For incompetent patients sustained by artificial life support with virtually no chance of recovery, courts have held that the life support may be withdrawn at the request of the incompetent patient's guardians when there is sufficient evidence to establish that the patient, if competent, would have requested withdrawal. See *Matter of Quinlan* (N.J. 1976); *Matter of Quinlan* (N.J.1976); *Brophy v. New England Sinai Hospital, Inc.* (Mass.1986) and *Cruzan v. Director, Missouri Dept. of Health* (S.Ct. 1990). (In *Cruzan*, the Supreme Court recognized the right of a person to refuse treatment, but held that a State may impose reasonable restrictions on that right, such as requiring the petitioners to establish the wishes of the now-incompetent patient by a higher standard of proof than a preponderance of the evidence.)

D. INFORMED CONSENT

The consent given by a patient to a health care provider must be the result of an informed decision. That is to say, certain information about the medical procedure, its risks and benefits, its costs and side effects, must be made available to the patient before consent is given. Informed consent is intended to give the patient the information needed in order for him or her to make a decision that reflects the wishes of the patient. This provides the patient with autonomy and self-determination. Courts have recognized that informed consent involves more than simply obtaining the signature of a patient on a form. It is, in effect, a process, involving a dialogue between the health care provider and the patient. For example, in a discussion of the nature of informed consent, the Maryland court said in *Sard v. Hardy* (Md.1977):

> The doctrine of informed consent . . . follows logically from the universally recognized rule that a physician, treating a mentally competent adult under non-emergency circumstances, cannot properly undertake to perform surgery or administer other therapy without the prior consent of his patient. In order for the patient's consent to be effective, it must have been an "informed consent," one that is given after the patient has received a fair and reasonable explanation of the contemplated treatment or procedure.

It follows that if the health care provider does not make the necessary disclosures and does not receive the patient's "informed consent," he or she is exposed to liability for malpractice.

The doctrine of informed consent is a limited one but there are signs that courts are beginning to expand this claim. The information necessary for a patient to decide whether to consent to a medical procedure expands beyond the actual procedure, and can include the personal characteristics and experience of the physician. For instance a physician's experience level could be a material factor when considering a particularly difficult or specialized operation. If a patient cannot weigh this factor when assessing the risk of the procedure being consented to, then a lack of informed consent claim may be made. *See Howard v. University of Med. & Dentistry of New Jersey* (N.J.2002)(plaintiff was allowed to amend his complaint to include an informed consent claim when plaintiff learned that, despite defendants own contentions, defendant was not a board certified neurosurgeon and had performed a type of surgery only a couple dozen times rather than the sixty he claimed to have performed). The Supreme Court of Pennsylvania disagrees with this approach. In *Duttry v. Patterson* (Pa.2001), where the surgeon misinformed the plaintiff regarding the number of previous procedures he had performed, the court held that information "of a physician's personal characteristics and experience" is irrelevant to the doctrine of informed consent.

III. INFORMED REFUSAL OF TREATMENT

A patient has the right to refuse, as well as consent, to treatment. The right to refuse treatment also has its roots in the right of self-determination and the right of privacy as interpreted through the first and fourteenth amendments to the Constitution. See also *In the Matter of Karen*

Quinlan (N.J.1976) (distinguishing homicide from right to terminate treatment in cases where patient is on artificial life-support).

Informed refusal of treatment requires that a physician communicate that information which a reasonable patient would require in order to make an "informed" judgment about whether to consent to treatment. Such information includes the risks and benefits of a proposed treatment, as well as the available alternatives. Furthermore, as part of the physician-patient relationship, the physician also has an obligation to disclose to the patient the consequences of failing to undergo a recommended medical procedure, and can be held liable in malpractice if he fails to do so.

In *Truman v. Thomas* (Cal.1980) a family practitioner recommended that a female patient of childbearing age undergo a routine pap smear, which tests for cervical cancer. Although he claims to have offered the procedure to his patient on several occasions, he never specifically advised her about the benefits of the procedure, and particularly the risks of failing to have the test. The patient refused the test, allegedly because of its cost, and later died of cervical cancer. The California Supreme Court held the physician liable on the basis that he failed to disclose a material risk of refusing the recommended procedure. In defining "material risk" the court identified that information "which the physician knows or should know would be regarded as significant by a reasonable person in the patient's position when deciding to accept or reject the recommended medical procedure." In *Curtis v. Jaskey* (Ill.App.2001) the plaintiff, while in prenatal care, explicitly told the physician not to perform an episiotomy during childbirth. However, during the delivery, the defendant performed such procedure claiming an emergency exception, thus not requiring the patient's consent. The Illinois Appeals Court disagreed, finding that the patient had intended the refusal to apply in the circumstances that procedure was rendered. Furthermore, the court held the emergency exception was inapplicable. *Id.*

Generally, when a medical condition is not life-threatening, a patient has a right to refuse treatment, or choose a procedure other than that recommended, assuming the patient is competent to do so. There are exceptions to this rule, which are beyond the scope of this discussion. Generally, the exceptions apply to the treatment of children whose parent(s) or guardian refuse to consent to recommended procedures, and to competent adults whose medical conditions pose a grave risk to life. In the latter, some courts have been willing to balance the right of the patient to refuse treatment with the right of a minor child, for example, whose well-being would be significantly affected by the death of a parent. In *Norwood Hospital v. Munoz* (Mass. 1991) and *Public Health Trust of Dade County v. Wons* (Fla.1989) competent adult patients, who were Jehovah's Witnesses, refused life-saving blood transfusions on the basis that receiving blood products was contrary to their religious beliefs. The courts held that the right of such adults to refuse lifesaving treatment was not absolute, but would be considered in light of other interests which the state was obligated to promote. Such interests included the rights of their minor children to preserve a parent's life, and in each case the patient's right to refuse treatment *was* overridden. Cases such as *Munoz* and *Wons* are the exception, however, and typically an informed patient may refuse treatment, even when his or her condition is life-threatening. In emergency situations and those in which the competency of the patient is uncertain, physicians may err on the side of providing treatment. Providing treatment in a life-threatening situation to a patient who has expressed their lack of consent for religious reasons is a much more sensitive issue. In *In re Duran* (Pa.Super.2001) the patient, a Jehovah's Witness, appointed a health care agent and signed a durable power of attorney stating that because of her religious beliefs she refused all types of blood transfusions, even if her life depended on it. Duran went into a coma and her husband petitioned the court to intervene. The husband was appointed guardian and was successful in having the transfusion performed even though the patient died shortly thereafter. The health care agent appealed on public policy grounds to establish the individual's right to refuse medical treatment especially where a health care agent was appointed. The appeals court balanced Duran's religious beliefs and her refusal of treatment against the state's interest in protecting third parties and held that "absent evidence of overarching state interests, the patient's clear and unequivocal wishes should generally be accepted." *Id.*

IV. THE DUTY OF DISCLOSURE

Although it is clear that the patient is entitled to obtain the information necessary to give an informed consent, the question sometimes arises as to who has the obligation to make the necessary disclosures. In particular, when more than one health care provider is involved, it is not always clear with whom the duty to disclose ultimately rests. In general, most courts will hold that the duty of disclosure remains with the physician who performs the medical procedure or provides the medical treatment, diagnostic tests or other medical care. See Rozovsky, Consent to Treatment: A Practical Guide, 2nd Ed. (Little, Brown & Co.1990); *Ritter v. Delaney* (Tex.App.1990). The health care facility is not generally responsible for obtaining informed consent unless it knew or had reason to know that the physician had not obtained the patient's consent. *Rozovsky* at 69. See also *Pauscher v. Iowa Methodist Med. Center* (Iowa 1987).

In cases where multiple physicians participate in the treatment of a patient, it is not always clear where the duty to obtain informed consent should lie. For example, if a physician requests a consultation and the consulting physician requires that certain tests be performed, generally it is only the consultant that is required to obtain consent. On the other hand, if a physician orders a procedure to be performed by another physician (such as a radiologist), it is possible that both physicians may incur the duty to obtain consent. See *Halley v. Birbiglia* (Mass.1983). The question of whether both physicians are responsible depends largely upon whether the second physician acted in the capacity of an assistant, or whether he was responsible for a discrete aspect of the treatment. Cf. *Cornfeldt v. Tongen* (Minn.1977) (anesthesiologist and general surgeon both responsible for disclosure to the patient) with *Bell v. Umstattd* (Tex.App. 1966) (anesthesiologist not responsible for disclosure to the patient unless the patient makes specific inquiry of him). Still other courts defer to the applicable standards of the profession to determine who has an obligation of disclosure.

A. STANDARDS FOR DISCLOSURE

The law of informed consent must necessarily apply a standard to determine whether or not a physician provided the patient with enough information when the patient's consent was sought and obtained. Historically, the test was the "professional standard" as articulated in the leading case of *Natanson v. Kline* (Kan.1960). In *Natanson*, the court stated that the duty to disclose was "limited to those disclosures which a reasonable medical practitioner would make under the same or similar circumstances." In applying this standard, the plaintiff must present expert testimony from other physicians to show that the defendant did not provide as much information as a reasonable physician would have provided in the same situation. See *Culbertson v. Mernitz* (Ind.1992). The "same situation" requirement has been interpreted with some specificity. For example, some jurisdictions hold that if a doctor is practicing in a small town, he or she should only be held to the standard of doctors practicing in small towns, not large cities. See *Smith v. Weaver* (Neb.1987) and West's Neb.Rev.St. §§ 44–2801 et seq., 44–2816 (2003). With the advent of a more universal quality of health care, regardless of location, this specificity requirement may be diminishing.

The majority of jurisdictions apply the professional standard test to informed consent cases. However, a minority of states apply the "material risk" or "reasonable patient" standard. This standard was adopted in such cases as *Canterbury v. Spence* (D.C.Cir.1972) and *Cobbs v. Grant* (Cal.1972). See also *Largey v. Rothman* (N.J.1988) and *Hondroulis v. Schuhmacher* (La.1988). In both *Canterbury* and *Cobbs*, the courts found that the professional standard violated the patient's right of self-determination. The patient owns the right to determine what is to be done with his or her body. Thus, the focus should be on what information the patient requires to make a decision, rather than on what a reasonable physician would do under the circumstances. *Canterbury* held that in order for a patient to give informed consent, he or she must have all the "material" information regarding "the inherent and potential hazards of the proposed treatment, the alternatives to that treatment, if any, and the results likely if the patient remains untreated."

The *Canterbury* court defined materiality as follows:

A risk is thus material when a reasonable person, in what the physician knows or should know to be the patient's position, would be likely to attach significance to the risk or cluster of risks in deciding whether or not to forego the proposed therapy.

The test these courts applied is an objective test. In order for the plaintiff to prevail, she must establish that she would not have consented to the procedure had she been given sufficient information and that a reasonable person would likewise have refused.

Since the adoption of the material risk standard, the courts have struggled with the application of the materiality test to fact patterns being litigated. Two factors the courts have weighed are the severity of the undisclosed risk and the incidence of harm. A consensus appears to be developing that the greater the severity, the more likely the risk should be disclosed, even if the incidence of the materialized risk is small. See *Jaskoviak v. Gruver* (N.D. 2002) (explaining expert testimony often used to establish risk and its likelihood of occurrence).

B. EXCEPTIONS TO THE
DUTY TO DISCLOSE

In certain situations physicians have a right to proceed with treatment in the absence of the informed consent of the patient. The three major exceptions that occur concern *(1) emergency, (2) waiver and (3) therapeutic privilege.*

The common law recognizes the right of a doctor to act with out patient consent in true emergency situations, so long as he conforms to customary emergency practices. See *Jackovach v. Yocom* (Iowa 1931). In the event of a medical emergency, a physician is expected to render life-saving care to a patient whether the patient or a close relative is present to consent to treatment. A medical emergency is present when the life of the patient is threatened or when the failure to perform a certain procedure will reasonably result in a serious or permanent impairment or disfigurement to the patient. The patient is said to impliedly consent to treatment until such time as his or her condition is stabilized. See implied consent, supra at pp. 100 and the Good Samaritan statutes at pp. 156–160.

The patient's right to informed consent might also be waived under certain limited circumstances. Under limited circumstances, some courts may consider that a patient has waived his right to informed consent in situations such as: (1) when a patient determines that he understands little about the medical procedure in question, and is in no position to make an informed judgement; or (2) is under such stress that he is unable to make an informed judgement; or (3) a language barrier exists that can not be overcome by translation. It is generally not acceptable, however, for a patient to blindly assert that he will not or cannot participate in the decision about whether to accept treatment, leaving the physician to act on his own. Furthermore, "[t]o waive the right of informed consent the patient must know he has the right. The patient needs to be aware of the doctor's duty to disclose, the patient's own right to make a decision either consenting or refusing, and that the doctor cannot do anything without his consent." Burwell, Informed Consent, 34 Med. Tr. Tech. Q. 439 (1988).

A concept known as "therapeutic privilege" is available in limited circumstances. The therapeutic privilege gives a physician the right to withhold information that is pertinent to informed decision-making because the physician believes that disclosure itself would harm the patient. Thus, if it reasonably appears that the required disclosure might so upset the patient that it would threaten his or her health or well-being, the physician may have the right to withhold such information or limit the scope of such information.

The standard for invoking the therapeutic privilege is a "reasonable practitioner" standard. See *Nishi v. Hartwell* (Haw.1970). In *Canterbury v. Spence* (D.C.Cir.1972), the court held that the therapeutic privilege is only be appropriate in such cases where it appears that the risk of disclosure poses such a detrimental threat to the patient as to become infeasible or contraindicated from a medical point of view. *Id. Canterbury* also noted that even when the privilege is invoked, the physician must still provide the patient with information that is relevant and not harmful to the patient. Thus it is not a blanket privilege. See also *Salgo v. Leland Stanford Jr. University Board of Trustees* (Cal.App. 1957).

Finally, a recent federal court held that under a particular circumstance where obtaining informed consent was "not feasible", the requirement would not be imposed. In *Doe v. Sullivan* (D.C.Cir.1991) the plaintiff alleged that the government, without informed consent, used unapproved investigational drugs on military personnel stationed in Saudi Arabia during the Gulf War. The court held that it would be impractical to obtain consent from all combat-ready personnel, and thus the informed consent requirement was not enforceable. This exception to the rule would not likely extend to situations not involving military readiness.

C.   DUTY TO DISCLOSE ECONOMIC INTERESTS

A health care provider has a duty to disclose medical information to the patient, as well as, other types of information in certain situations. Recently, courts have held that physicians have a duty to disclose any economic interest that a physician might have in a patient's tissue. This matter was discussed in the landmark case of *Moore v. Regents of The University of California* (Cal.1990). The plaintiff in this case had a rare form of cancer known as hair-cell leukemia. Because this disease was so rare, the plaintiff's cells and blood product was of great commercial value. During the ongoing doctor/patient relationship, the doctors were profiting financially by the use of the plaintiff's cells without ever revealing this to the plaintiff. Informed consent was neither sought nor given. The plaintiff sued on the theory of conversion, breach of fiduciary duty and lack of informed consent. The court held that the doctor had a fiduciary duty to his patient and that informed consent should have been sought by the doctors before entering into any activities in which they would profit from plaintiff's cells. But it also ruled that there was no cause of action for conversion, saying that patients do not own the tissue removed from their bodies and have no right to share in the profits from the commercialization of such tissue.

D. EXPERIMENTAL PROCEDURES

Courts hold that when a health care provider offers and experimental procedure to a patient, the provider has a duty to inform the patient of the experimental nature of the proposed procedure. See *Torsch v. McLeod* (Ala.1995) (affirming $3 million award). In *Torsch*, the physician's estate was held liable for implanting an intraocular lens into the patient's blind eye without getting her consent to use the device and without disclosing the experimental nature of the procedure.

E. HIV STATUS OF THE PHYSICIAN

With the growth of the AIDS epidemic, doctors have been forced to consider, as an issue of informed consent, their duty to disclose their own HIV status in cases that it might reasonably impact a patient's decision making. Physicians who are seropositive for HIV are faced with the decision of revealing to their HIV status to their patients. In the case of *Faya v. Almaraz* (Md.1993), the court held a surgeon with AIDS had a legal duty to his patients to inform them of his condition before operating. In *Faya*, the surgeon performed breast surgery on two female patients at a time he knew he was HIV positive. The court reasoned that there was a foreseeable harm that the patient might contract the AIDS virus during the invasive surgery. Other courts have followed *Faya*, finding that a physician with the HIV virus does have a duty to disclose his or her HIV status. See *Doe v. Noe* (Ill.App.1997).

The duty to disclose information regarding the HIV virus developed in the mid–1980's. A court held that a physician had no duty to disclose to a patient the risk of contracting the HIV virus from a blood transfusion prior to 1985 because such a risk was not apparent before then. The court also held that the physician had no duty to inform the patient about alternatives, such as autologous transfusion or self-donation. See *Doe v. Johnston* (Iowa 1991).

F. AFTER–DISCOVERED DANGERS

Doctors may also have a duty to disclose after discovered dangers. That is, if a doctor discovers after a procedure that a patient might be at risk, the doctor has a duty to disclose such information. See *Tresemer v. Barke* (Cal.App.1978) (gynecologist owed a duty to warn patient of dangers of intrauterine device, when doctor obtained new knowledge of its dangers).

V. THE REQUIREMENT OF CAUSATION

Once a plaintiff is able to establish that a physician acted, or failed to act, without the requisite consent, the plaintiff must still prove that the absence of informed consent is causally related to an identifiable harm. Like all negligence actions, those premised upon failure of informed consent also require proof of causation. In general, the plaintiff must establish that had the necessary information been provided, he or she would have acted differently or expected a different outcome.

In determining whether a different outcome would have occurred had the required information been disclosed, a number of different "tests" or "standards" have been used. A majority of jurisdictions use an objective or "reasonable person" standard. The reasonable person standard requires the plaintiff to establish that the reasonable person, having been given the necessary information, would have refused (or accepted) the proposed treatment.

See Rozovsky, Consent to Treatment: A Practical Guide, 2nd Ed. (Little, Brown & Co.1990) at 79. See also *Pardy v. United States* (7th Cir.1986).

An alternative to the objective test is the "subjective" or "actual patient" test. Those jurisdictions which apply this standard would allow a particular plaintiff to establish that although the reasonable person might not have acted differently had the necessary information been disclosed, he or she would have on the basis of some individual character or personality trait or experience. See *Arena v. Gingrich* (Or.1988). The standard of proof can vary, but proof of a subjective reason for believing that one would act contrary to that of the reasonable person might require clear and convincing evidence.

Yet another alternative is for the court to require that both the objective and subjective standards be satisfied. This might minimize the likelihood that a patient, observing through hindsight, would opt for a different result. See *Harnish v. Children's Hospital* (Mass.1982). If both standards are required a plaintiff must prove, that even if the reasonable person would have acted in a particular way, the patients would have acted differently. The outcome-determinative element of causation, particularly when observed on an objective basis, makes it difficult to establish that the absence of informed consent "caused" the patient's injury.

Many courts require a further element of causation when a patient alleges that a risk of a certain treatment was not adequately disclosed, and that had disclosure been made, the procedure would have been refused. They require that the risk complained of actually materialize. See *Canterbury v. Spence* (D.C.Cir.1972). In *Canterbury*, the physician allegedly failed to disclose that paralysis was a risk of a laminectomy procedure, and that failure to disclose that risk violated the physician's duty of care. Furthermore, had such a risk been disclosed, the patient alleged that he would have refused the procedure. After the procedure, the plaintiff was paralyzed, and the physician was held liable.

Finally, courts generally require that any injury that results after nondisclosure of a material risk be proximately caused by the medical treatment or procedure. Thus if paralysis is a material risk of a laminectomy procedure, and paralysis results, it must still be proved that it was the laminectomy that caused the paralysis.

VI. FRAUDULENT MISREPRESENTATION AND CONCEALMENT

Properly obtained informed consent can become void if it was obtained by fraudulent misrepresentation, concealment or non-disclosure of information by the doctor. An action for intentional misrepresentation may be maintained if (1) a false statement of material fact is made; (2) the misrepresentation is made by a party who knows or believes the statement is false; (3) the party intends to induce another to act; (4) action by the other is made in reliance on the statement's truth; and (5) injury to the patient results from said reliance. *Smith v. Kurtzman* (Ill.App.1988). The requirements for a successful action to void consent based on misrepresentation are substantially the same as for ordinary negligence cases except that in the former, the act is done intentionally. See *Bloskas v. Murray* (Colo. 1982).

In another case, a California court held that a professional football player had been the victim of misrepresentation. The player suffered a knee injury while in college and re-injured the knee during his professional career. The team doctor failed to reveal to him that he had a degenerative and irreversible knee injury and that continued professional play would only worsen the condition. See Restatement (Second) of Torts §§ 310–311, 525, 550, 552.

CHAPTER FIVE

CAUSATION AND DAMAGES

I. IN GENERAL: ESTABLISHING CAUSATION

A cause of action for negligence requires four elements: a duty that exists to the plaintiff based upon a standard of care; breach of that duty; a proximate and causal connection between the breach and the plaintiff's injury causation; and damages. See Chapter 2. On the other hand, it is often said that a practitioner is negligent when he fails to adhere to the requisite standard of care. The distinction is that in order to maintain an actionable claim, the negligent act must also be causally related to an identifiable harm. The element of causation along with the existence of damages transforms substandard practice into an actionable negligence claim.

The fact that there must be a causal connection between the substandard level of care and the harm that results is undisputed. The absence of such a connection will be fatal to a claim of malpractice. Thus in *Alfonso v. Lund* (10th Cir.1986) in which the plaintiff claimed that his two fingers which had been accidentally severed could have been re-implanted, the court held that the plaintiff must demonstrate the defendant's actions proximately caused the disability and disfigurement that he alleges: "The burden of proving with reasonable certainty the causal connection between the treatment complained of and the plaintiff's loss or injury rests on the plaintiff, and a judgment in a malpractice action based upon conjecture, surmise or speculation cannot be sustained...." See also *Paige v. Manuzak* (Md.App.1984) in which the court refused to hold a hospital liable for negligently administering penicillin post-operatively to an allergic patient because there was no proof that subsequent complications were proximately caused by the negligent use of the drug.

It is often said that there are two types of causation: cause-in-fact and proximate cause. If injury to the plaintiff would not have occurred "but for" the defendant's wrongful act, or if injury to the plaintiff was a foreseeable result of the defendant's act, it is said that the acts of the defendant were the cause-in-fact of the plaintiff's injury. Proximate cause, on the other hand, refers to whether, considering all other relevant factors, the act(s) of the defendant were the legal cause of the plaintiff's injury. For example, the defendant's act(s) may have been one factor but not necessarily the only factor. Proximate cause in that instance may depend upon whether the act(s) of the defendant were a significant factor in bringing about the plaintiff's injury. Alternatively, the acts of one person might set into motion certain events, but another's act might constitute a superseding cause which results in the plaintiff's injury. Thus the cause-in-fact is an important determination, but ultimately it is the proximate cause that determines the liability of the defendant.

Negligent acts and omissions may be said to be the cause of injury if they satisfy the "but for" test. Thus if it can be said that *but for* the acts of the defendant, the plaintiff would not have sustained his injury, the defendant's actions were a cause of injury. On the other hand, the fact that the actions were a cause of injury might not result in his liability unless it is established that they were a substantial cause of injury. The New Hampshire case of *Peterson v. Gray* (N.H.1993) highlights the difficulty in using proximate cause as a determining factor for establishing liability. In that case a plaintiff with a preexisting condition engaged the defendant to perform hand surgery, but did not achieve a successful result. The court observed that " ... if the jury determined that the plaintiff's [pre-existing condition] was 'a proximate cause' of [her result], then the defendant's actions could not possibly have been 'the proximate cause.' "

A. CONTRIBUTING FACTOR

In *Mitchell v. Gonzales* (Cal.1991) the California Supreme Court rejected jury instructions on proximate cause on the basis that they were unduly confusing to the jury. Instead, it relied on whether the conduct of the defendant was a "contributing factor" to the plaintiff's injury. This goes beyond the "substantial factor" principles, but indicates that causation is not necessarily an all-or-nothing matter. The trier of fact must then determine the extent to which the act contributed to the plaintiff's injury in deciding whether the defendant should be held liable.

B.   SUPERSEDING CAUSE

In some cases the harm to a patient may have multiple causes, at least as determined by the "but for" test. For example, in *Siggers v. Barlow* (6th Cir.1990) an emergency room physician negligently diagnosed the plaintiff, failing to identify a fracture that required surgery. When the x-ray films were read by an attending physician, the fracture was identified and reported to a subsequent emergency room physician whose duty was to communicate the new diagnosis to the patient. The patient was never notified and suffered irreparable injury as a result. The court noted that under the applicable law the question of whether the "superseding cause" constituted a legal cause was one for the court (as opposed to the jury) to determine. A superseding cause is defined as "an act of a third person or other force which by its intervention prevents the actor from being liable for harm to another which his antecedent negligence is a substantial factor in bringing about." Restatement (Second) of Torts § 440. The court concluded that the failure of a third person to prevent the harm caused by another person's negligence is not a superseding cause.

Other courts have used the "Intervening Cause" doctrine as a common-law device to shift liability from the original negligent actor to an intervening actor who brings about a new, unforeseen harm. The doctrine provides that the original negligent actor will be relieved from liability when a new, independent and unforeseen cause intervenes to produce a result that could not have been foreseen. The Intervening Cause doctrine applies when three conditions are met: (1) the intervening act was sufficient by itself to cause the injury; (2) the intervening act was not reasonably foreseeable by the negligent actor; and (3) the negligent act was not a normal response to the original negligent actor's conduct. The underlying theory behind the use of this doctrine is that an independent, intervening causation breaks the chain of legal causation between the original tortfeasor's conduct and the eventual injury. See, e.g. *Waste Management v. South Central Bell Telephone* (Tenn.App.1997). But see, *Chamberland v. Roswell Osteopathic Clinic* (N.M.App.2001) the court reasoned that an instruction on independent intervening cause was not appropriate in a case of failure to diagnose appendicitis because an independent intervening cause instruction assumes negligence and causation in fact. Therefore, without an original tortious action or omission committed by the clinic staff resulting in the appendicitis, subsequent causes cannot intervene.

C. JOINT AND SEVERAL LIABILITY

Sometimes an injury is caused by the negligent acts of two or more persons who act in concert, resulting in the plaintiff's injury. If it appears that they acted together (rather than separately) and in so doing caused a single injury, they are usually considered to be "joint tortfeasors." The determination about whether to assess liability jointly is a decision for the trial court, and is likely to depend upon such factors as whether each defendant had a similar duty, whether the same facts and evidence will be used in the cases against each of them, and whether the injury to the plaintiff can be separated into aspects caused by each tortfeasor. See, e.g. *Riff v. Morgan Pharmacy* (Pa.Super.1986).

In the medical context, the alternative to practitioners acting together to cause injury to the plaintiff is the possibility that they act successively. In such a case the subsequent practitioner might have either mitigated the damage of the first or corrected the problem before the patient suffered damages. For example, one physician might be negligent in his initial diagnosis or treatment of a problem, and a subsequent practitioner fails to identify and correct it, perhaps resulting in an exacerbation of the original symptoms. Who is liable, and for what?

The first practitioner who was negligent in diagnosing and treating the problem is potentially liable not only for all foreseeable consequences as a result of his own negligence, but also for the foreseeable consequences of the negligence of the subsequent practitioner. See 1 D. Louisell and H. Williams, Medical Malpractice 16.06 (1986). When there are successive acts of negligence by two or more tortfeasors, they are generally considered to be co-tortfeasors under statutes calling for contribution among tortfeasors. See *Foote v. United States* (N.D.Ill. 1986).

What happens when two or more tortfeasors act together to cause a single harm? In most jurisdictions each of the individual tortfeasors is liable to the plaintiff for the entire harm. The liability is considered to be both "joint" (both are liable together) and "several" (each are liable for the entire judgment individually). This enables the plaintiff to recover from either tortfeasor, or both tortfeasors for the entire amount, except that the plaintiff is only entitled to recover until he or she has been fully compensated. No double recoveries are permitted. This is because once the plaintiff's judgment has been satisfied in full from one tortfeasor, that tortfeasor is entitled to seek contribution from the other, usually in the amount of one-half (assuming two tortfeasors) of the judgment. In the few jurisdictions that do not recognize joint and several liability, usually the court will apportion the defendants' liability according to their relative fault, and thereafter the plaintiff must recover from each only what the court has apportioned. Apportionment may also be available in those jurisdiction that do impose joint and several liability, but one or more defendants are able to carry the burden of reasonably apportioning the damages attributable to each defendant.

D. LOSS OF A CHANCE

Another difficult situation occurs when more than one influence comes together to contribute to a plaintiff's injury. One possibility is that the plaintiff in some way contributed to his own condition, for example, by neglecting to follow the physician's instructions. Another possibility is that the plaintiff had a "preexisting condition," i.e. a medical condition that occurred or existed prior to the acts of the defendant that affected the plaintiff's outcome in a significant way. In the event that there is a preexisting condition, the next inquiry is whether it affected the outcome of the physician's treatment, including negligent treatment. For example, a plaintiff has an inoperable and thus terminal cancer, and is administered a drug to which he is allergic for an unrelated condition. The patient dies of the allergic reaction. The terminal cancer is not relevant to the defendant's liability for the wrongful death, even though the value of the plaintiff's life might be diminished by its quality and life expectancy. In other cases, of course, the preexisting condition is directly related to the treatment that is negligently administered.

The liability of the defendant for the harm caused to a plaintiff with a preexisting condition depends upon how his negligence contributes to the plaintiff's harm. If the negligence results in the worsening of the condition or in the exacerbation of harmful consequences, he is likely to be liable for the increased harm, but not for the preexisting condition. On the other hand, if the negligence of the physician results in the loss of a possible opportunity for recovery or survival, courts differ on when "loss of a chance" becomes a compensable injury. If, for example, the plaintiff had a small chance of recovery from a certain condition, and the negligence of the defendant deprived the plaintiff of that chance, the question of whether that chance supports a compensable loss is not addressed uniformly by the courts.

In *Boody v. United States* (D.Kan.1989) the plaintiff died after a tumor on her lung, which the defendant failed to diagnose, metastasized and spread to her brain. There was expert testimony that had the tumor been diagnosed in its early stage, there was a 51% chance that she would have lived for five years; after the metastasis, there was a very slight chance for survival. Consistent with a growing trend, the federal court specifically rejected the idea that a plaintiff can recover for a loss-of-a-chance only if the probability of a favorable outcome was greater than fifty per cent. Rather, the court adopted what is now a majority rule that loss-of-a-chance means loss of an "appreciable" chance which depends upon the circumstances of the case. In *Boody*, a 51% chance of surviving for five years was considered an "appreciable" chance. See also *Herskovits v. Group Health Cooperative of Puget Sound* (Wash.1983) in which the court held that evidence of a reduction in the chance of survival from 39% to 25% was sufficient to go to the jury on the issue of proximate cause; *Bird v. Saenz* (Cal.

App.2001) where the California Court of Appeals reversed the trial court's holding that loss of chance was not a valid claim because "the defendant did not have more then a 50% chance of survival prior to the alleged malpractice." In remanding the case to the trial court, the appellate court reasoned the defendant's negligent treatment for the plaintiff's cancer created new complications that were contributing factors in bringing about her death. *Roberts v. Ohio Permanente Med Group* (Ohio 1996) further supported the holding in *Boody* when the court overruled previous case law that rejected the loss of chance doctrine. The Ohio court held that a patient who had suffered a 17 month delay in the diagnosis of lung cancer and had less than a 50% chance of survival had a valid claim under the loss of chance doctrine. Similarly, in *Jorgenson v. Vener* (S.D. 2000) the South Dakota Supreme Court recognized the loss of chance doctrine upon a doctors failure to diagnose a chronic bone infection and to refer the plaintiff to an infectious disease specialist. The Supreme Court reasoned that the loss of chance doctrine "properly balance[d] the competing concerns of a patient who receives negligent treatment, against those of the doctor who practices the inexact science of medicine." In contrast, *Grant v. American Nat. Red Cross*, (D.C.App.2000) refused to apply the loss of chance standard, allowing summary judgment where the "plaintiff could not prove by greater than 50% that he would not have been injured but for the defendant's act". The court stated that the loss of chance standard should be applied to cases where the performance of a medical procedure would make the likelihood of success greater if the procedure were carried out.

Once a court finds that the loss-of-a-chance of survival is a compensable injury, the next inquiry concerns how to value that chance. While there continues to be controversy in this area, the most reasoned approach would appear to restore to the plaintiff that which was lost: the likelihood of having survived multiplied by the value of what was lost. Thus if the chance of survival that was lost due to the negligence of the defendant was 40% that the plaintiff would have lived for five years, the plaintiff should presumably recover 40% of the value of five years of life. In so doing, damages are apportioned directly in relation to the harm that has been caused. More importantly, it eliminates the inequity of depriving plaintiffs of any compensation for the loss-of-chance when they are unable to establish with any certainty that their chance of survival in the absence of the defendant's negligence was at least 50 per cent.

E. ESTABLISHING PROXIMATE CAUSE

In most medical malpractice actions the burden of proof rests with the plaintiff who must establish by a preponderance of the evidence that the defendant's act was the cause of the harm suffered. The "preponderance of the evidence" standard is the lowest one used in civil actions; it means only that it is "more likely than not" that the plaintiff should prevail. It is also sometimes called the "51%" standard. In essence, it reflects the inherent uncertainty of jury verdicts, and the fact that they are often issued based upon probabilities that fault really existed. In reconstructing factual situations it often is not possible to be certain about what happened or why, but only to speculate and assign a probability to its accuracy. If the probability is greater than 50%, it is *more probable than not.*

In the great majority of medical malpractice cases the element of causation must be proved by expert testimony. Since most medical occurrences are not within the common knowledge of the lay jury, expert testimony enables the jury to understand the standard of care, any departures from that standard along with causation and damages. Of course, it requires the jury to make some judgments about the credibility of the expert witnesses and the evidence that they rely upon, but without their assistance the lay jury could do no more than speculate about matters far beyond their possible comprehension.

There are several possible exceptions to the need for expert testimony which have been discussed in depth in Chapter 2. These include situations in which the act or occurrence, as well as its causative effects, are within the general knowledge of the lay jury. They also include situations in which the defendant, through his own testimony, admissions and other credible evidence is able to provide the necessary expert analysis. Sometimes they include circumstances in which a defendant, having violated a pertinent statute or ordinance, might be presumed to have been negligent. And finally, they may include those situations in which the plaintiff has no knowledge of how or what caused his injury, but the injury is such that it usually does not generally occur in the absence of negligence. With the aid of the doctrine of *res ipsa loquitur*, the plaintiff may be able to secure a permissible inference of negligence, sufficient to get to the jury. If the elements of the doctrine are satisfied, the jury is entitled, but not required, to return a judgment for the plaintiff. For a discussion of these exceptions, see Chapter 2.

Because of the difficulty in making a definitive determination about whether a certain act proximately caused the plaintiff's injury, experts are usually asked to give their opinion about the probability that a certain medical event caused a certain outcome. Once again, questions arise about exactly how certain experts must be to make a judgment, and how the jury should evaluate a less-than-certain opinion. The traditional rule is that an expert is expected to state only those opinions which he is sure about "to a reasonable degree of medical certainty." The difficulty comes in deciding what this phrase means and how strictly the element of "reasonableness" should be interpreted. For example, one approach is to require that the direct and circumstantial evidence in the case (e.g., understanding of the particular subject matter, availability of requisite medical history and facts about the occurrence) allow the expert to form an opinion about the occurrence "to a reasonable degree of medical certainty." The alternative approach is to view the reasonable-degree-of-medical certainty as tantamount to carrying the ultimate burden of proof. Thus, the reasonable degree refers to whether it is "more likely than not" that the injury to the plaintiff was proximately caused by the negligence of the defendant. The second approach demonstrates the critical importance of expert testimony.

Medical malpractice cases often stand or fall on the opinions of the experts and the credibility assigned to their testimony. Some courts, however, reject the implicit conclusion of expert's testimony as being tantamount to a legal determination of proximate cause. Thus some trial courts will prevent the experts from purporting to testify as to the "ultimate issue" in a case, i.e., the determination of proximate cause. Such courts view proximate cause as a legal issue based upon a determination of all of the elements of the case: a duty of care, a breach of that duty, causation and damages. The role of the expert is to provide his medical opinion, but not to apply the law to the particular facts of the case. These courts may be troubled by the possibility that the jury would give undue weight to the ultimate conclusion of an expert who is willing to offer one. Other courts are willing to give limiting instructions to the jury which remind it that the opinions of the experts are just that: opinions, and it is the jury that ultimately makes the determination of liability.

II. DAMAGES

The final requisite element in proving a cause of action for medical malpractice is the determination that the plaintiff suffered a compensable harm as a result of the defendant's wrongful act. A plaintiff is required to prove the damages he has suffered as a basis for entitlement to equitable relief. The recovery of monetary damages is generally satisfied by showing that a "defendant's conduct caused some actual harm." See *Wright v. St. Mary's Med. Center, Inc.* (S.D.Ind.1999). The standard of proof required of a plaintiff to show damages is a fair preponderance of the evidence. See *Mead v. Wilson* (Conn.Super.2001). Two types of damages are potentially available: compensatory damages are intended to compensate the plaintiff for the actual harm suffered, including the pain and suffering of the plaintiff. Punitive damages are available in certain types of cases and are intended to punish a defendant who willfully or recklessly causes harm to a plaintiff. Restatement (Second) of Torts § 908(2) (date)

The nature of damages available in medical malpractice cases is governed, in large part, by the rules of personal injury practice of the jurisdiction. Plaintiffs who sustain their burden of proof for tort claims can recover out-of-pocket losses (medical bills and future medical expense), loss of income and temporary or permanent impairment of earning capacity, incidental expenses, and recovery of an amount of money that fairly represents the pain, suffering and mental distress of the injured plaintiff. But see, *Bynum v. Magno* (D.Haw.2000) in which the court denied plaintiff's wife's claim for loss of consortium following the couple's divorce, even though the couple apparently only divorced for financial reasons and remained loving and committed. The court reasoned "damages stemming from loss of consortium are limited to the period during which the spouses were married, regardless of their reason for divorce."

Plaintiffs who prove claims based upon breach of contract alleging that a practitioner promised a particular result or otherwise made a contractual promise may be entitled to a contract measure of damages. Damages for breach of contract can be measured by the value of the expectancy, the detrimental reliance caused by a promise, or an unjust enrichment of the defendant. See, generally, Chapter 9 for a discussion of contract remedies. Punitive (or "exemplary") damages are generally measured on the basis of what it takes to "punish" a grossly negligent, wilful or reckless tortfeasor, and a jury determination on that issue is often unpredictable. In some jurisdictions, punitive damages are expected to bear a relationship to the compensable damages, but in others substantial discretion is permitted.

III. SPECIFIC TYPES OF DAMAGE AWARDS

A. WRONGFUL LIFE AND WRONGFUL BIRTH

Claims for "wrongful life" or "wrongful birth" are typically brought when a physician negligently performs genetic testing, negligently fails to advise expectant parents that their child may be handicapped, or otherwise fails to act so that expectant parents can make an informed choice about whether to proceed with a pregnancy. Wrongful birth usually refers to a claim made by the parents of a handicapped child on the basis of the emotional distress and medical expenses to them; wrongful life is often a companion claim brought by the child who claims that *but for* the physician's negligence, he or she would not be impaired, or would not have been born at all. In yet other cases, (sometimes called "wrongful pregnancy" or "wrongful conception") a normal and healthy child is born, but one that was unintended and occurred as a result of negligence (e.g. negligent performance of a sterilization procedure.) In each case the question arises as to what, if any, damages are available to compensate the disappointed parents–or even the child.

Damages for claims of wrongful life, wrongful birth and even wrongful conception are not assessed uniformly among the jurisdictions. As a result, one should look to a specific jurisdiction's statutory and case law to determine what damages are generally awarded in these causes of action. In a growing number of cases for wrongful birth, courts have been willing to allow the jury to assess damages based upon the impairment to the lives of the parents, including extraordinary medical bills, disruptions to the family and emotional distress caused by the negligence. This presumes, of course, that the plaintiff is able to sustain the burden of proof that there was negligence on the part of the practitioner in failing to diagnose or treat a physical or genetic abnormality. It also presumes that the negligence results in the child's impairment or the parents' inability to opt for termination of the pregnancy.

In a case brought by the child for wrongful life, a few courts have been willing to compensate the child for expenses associated with the handicap, and even for the pain and suffering that the child must endure. However, a majority of courts have been unwilling to provide redress for the claim that a child's life of impairment makes him worse off than if he had never been born at all. Thus in those cases where the claim is that *but for* the physician's negligence the child would have been aborted, most courts are unwilling to engage in the difficult task of trying to compare the value of an impaired life to that of no life at all. Often (but not always) the result is that no damages are awarded for the "wrongful life." See *Lininger v. Eisenbaum* (Colo. 1988); *Kassama v. Magat* (Md. Ct. Spec. App. 2001), in refusing to recognize a claim for wrongful life the appeals court reasoned, "it is an impossible task to calculate damages based on a comparison between life in an impaired state and no life at all." A few courts have held to the contrary. See, e.g. *Procanik v. Cillo* (N.J.1984).

Probably the most difficult actions for calculating damages are those involving wrongful conception. When a normal and healthy child is born, courts differ in their approach to assessing damages against a negligent physician who, for example, failed to properly perform the sterilization procedure. A majority of such courts have awarded medical expenses that result from the physician's negligence (including the cost of sterilization), compensation for the parents' physical and mental pain and suffering and other consequential damages such as loss of wages. Occasionally punitive damages are available. On the other hand, ordinary child rearing expenses incurred as a result of the negligence are generally not recoverable, and many courts reach this conclusion by offsetting the amount recoverable by the parents by the so-called "benefits rule". This measures the presumed benefit to the parents of having a healthy child. It is measured in both pecuniary and non-pecuniary terms. See *C.S. v. Nielson* (Utah 1988); *Flint v. O'Connell* (Wis.App.2002) where the appeals court affirmed the lower courts holding that public policy prevented awarding damages for the birth of a healthy child. However, the appeals court reversed the lower courts decision as to the defendant's responsibility for the worsening of plaintiff's health resulting from the defendant's failure to diagnose the pregnancy.

B. DIGNITARY TORTS

Another area in which in has traditionally been difficult to measure damages is the so-called "torts of dignity." For example, in *Berthiaume's Estate v. Pratt* (Me.1976) a dying patient clearly indicated through hand and facial gestures that he objected to the taking of photographs of him which had no therapeutic value. The pictures were taken despite his objection. The court was willing to recognize potential liability of the hospital for invasion of the patient's right of privacy.

In another case, *Strachan v. John F. Kennedy Mem. Hosp.* (N.J.1988), the parents of a brain-dead 20–year-old boy were asked to consider donation of their son's organs. When they refused the hospital allegedly delayed disconnecting the life support system, hoping that the parents might be convinced to change their minds. It ultimately took three days between the determination of brain death and the termination of life support. In the parents' action against the hospital for negligent handling of a corpse and prevention of a proper burial the trial court awarded $140,000 for the mental suffering occasioned by tortious conduct. See also, *Estate of Taylor v. Muncie Med. Investors, L.P.* (Ind.App. 2000) the appeals court denied the plaintiff's claim for wrongful prolongation of life even though the deceased had executed a living will stating that if she was suffering from a terminal illness her doctors should not take "extraordinary means" to prolong her life. In opposition to the deceased's and her children's requests two separate doctors prolonged her life for over five months, however, the Indiana Court of Appeals refused to recognize the claim of wrongful termination of life.

The rules concerning dignitary torts vary widely among jurisdictions, as do the damages that might be awarded in such a case. Unlike typical negligence cases, however, a cause of action will generally lie for the harm caused, even if there is no physical injury. Generally claims of injury to dignity are intentional actions, and the damages that are recoverable reflect the emotional distress and suffering of the plaintiff.

C. HARM TO ONESELF

With increasing frequency claims are being lodged against health care professionals for the self-inflicted injuries of patients who prove to be a danger to themselves. Physicians who regularly attend psychiatric patients are often required to assess the dangerousness of the patient. In so doing, they must choose between involuntarily confining one who may pose a danger to himself and permitting his. The latter choice risks possible harm. Commitment decisions are made on the basis of the available information. A physician is not negligent merely because his judgment yields a bad result. If, however, he is negligent in his assessment of that information, an action against him may succeed. In *Widgeon v. Eastern Shore Hospital Center* (Md. 1984), supra, a man was involuntarily committed to a psychiatric facility on the basis of a false tale told by his wife. When he was brought in for examination, he demonstrated no "outward" signs of mental illness, but was confined anyway. The court held that when an individual is wrongly confined and thus deprived of a liberty interest, a cause of action is stated.

A physician may also be liable if he declines to confine a dangerous person who later inflicts injury on himself. The same standards of due care and negligence apply. A physician who acts unreasonably and in so doing fails to prevent a suicide or other self-destructive behavior may be liable for the consequences of his lack of due care. The difficulty that these cases present is assessing whether there was proximate cause between the negligence and the self-destructive acts. It Those acts that constitute a superseding cause arguably defeat liability. On the other hand, there is no negligence unless it was reasonably foreseeable that self-inflicted injury was a danger for that patient. The considered approach is to separate the issues of due care and proximate cause from those of cause-in-fact, since the cause-in-fact will usually be the patient's own actions.

D. PUNITIVE OR EXEMPLARY DAMAGES

The traditional rules governing personal injury actions for calculating damages are equally applicable in the medical malpractice context. Thus in addition to recovery for pecuniary losses, pain and suffering and emotional distress, there exists the possibility that a plaintiff may be entitled to punitive or exemplary damages. Such damages are considered when "... the act or omission complained of was the result of a conscious indifference to the right or welfare of the ... persons affected by it." *McPhearson v. Sullivan* (Tex.1971). The conduct must be more than merely negligent; it must be egregious or result from the willful, wanton or reckless conduct of the practitioner.

In *Jackson v. Taylor* (5th Cir.1990) the appellate court held that if the pleadings and evidence are sufficient to raise the issue of gross negligence, the court must submit a special question to the jury on the issue of exemplary damages. In *Jackson*, the plaintiff suffered from bleeding liver tumors as a result of birth control pills prescribed by the defendant. Expert testimony was presented concerning the defendant's standard of care which was described as grossly negligent. In particular, the record contained unrebutted information that the plaintiff had purchased over 1000 pills within a period that less than 200 were appropriate. The court found these facts were sufficient to raise the issue of gross negligence. Like all other elements of the plaintiff's case, gross negligence is generally proved on the basis of expert testimony which describes the extent of the breach of the applicable standard of due care.

IV. DAMAGE AWARDS AND MALPRACTICE REFORM

The law of medical malpractice developed rapidly in the 1970's and 1980's, with increases in both the theories of liability and the number of cases. Serious attention was required to reform the system, primarily to bring down the high cost of health care and the practice of medicine. Malpractice reform will be discussed in greater detail in Chapter 10?. Some reforms include statutory ceilings on the amount of damages that can be awarded in a particular care, as well as limitations on the contingent fees that lawyers can collect for extraordinary verdicts. Constitutional challenges have been raised in some states concerning damage limitations. Mechanisms of reform have not been uniform.

One of the most common limitations is a statutory cap on the amount of damages that can be awarded in a malpractice case. In some states such damage limitations have been held constitutional, as a legitimate means of furthering an important state interest i.e., addressing the medical malpractice crisis which is responsible, in part, for the exorbitant costs of health care. See, e.g., West's Ann. Ind. Code 16–9.5–2–2 (1984). In others, however, the distinction between damage caps in medical malpractice actions and other personal injury suits has led courts to hold such limitations to be unconstitutional as a violation of the equal protection of the laws. See Vernon's Ann.Tex.Civ. Stat. arts. 4590, 5511.02, 11.04 (Supp. 1985). update

Another avenue of reform of medical malpractice litigation is the availability of additional compensation to a plaintiff from collateral sources. In general, the rule is that a plaintiff who protects himself from loss by carrying insurance or receives compensation from other "collateral" sources does not reduce the obligation of a wrongdoer by deducting from his recovery the amount received from a collateral source. As between an innocent plaintiff and a culpable wrongdoer, the plaintiff yields the benefit of the additional, collateral source. Some states have attempted to abrogate the common law rule in cases of medical malpractice (specifically insurance payments) in order to reduce the overall damage awards. Of those, some, but not others, have found the abrogation of the common law to be constitutional. See *Fein v. Permanente Medical Group* (Cal. 1985) (holding such a statute constitutional.) See also *Doran v. Priddy* (D.Kan.1981).

The medical malpractice "crisis" which formally took hold in the mid–1970's reaches greater and greater proportions each year. As a result, many of the proposed reforms of health care have focused on reforming the litigation system and limiting the damages that can be awarded for medical injuries. See Chapter 10. Many proposals exists, from creating a "no-fault" system for medical accidents to overhauling the jury system to further limiting the amount of recovery available to victims. In each case the challenge is to balance a fair system of compensation for victims with one that provides an incentive for a high standard of medical care.

CHAPTER SIX

AFFIRMATIVE DEFENSES, LIMITATIONS AND IMMUNITIES

I. IN GENERAL: STATUTES OF LIMITATIONS

Statutes of limitations are generally enacted to limit the amount of time in which a plaintiff can bring a cause of action against an alleged wrongdoer. The goal of these statutes is to balance the needs of the plaintiff to have a reasonable period of time to bring an action with those of the defendant who would otherwise be subject to potential liability for an indefinite period of time. Additionally, the statutes serve to avoid overburdening the judicial system with stale claims that are difficult to establish because evidence may be lost and the memories of credible witnesses fade. A number of states have a separate statute of limitations for medical malpractice actions. A court's decision as to whether a particular malpractice action is brought within the applicable limitations period depends upon the length of the period as defined by the statute, and any factors that might serve to toll the running of the limitations period. See, e.g., Bonin v. Vannaman (Kan.1996)(8 year statute of repose for persons under a legal disability not inconsistent with due process or equal protection); but cf. Makos v. Wisconsin Masons Health Care Fund (Wis.1997)(5 year statute of repose unconstitutional where patient did not discover misdiagnosis until four years after expiration of limitations period.)

A. STANDARD RULES FOR ACCRUAL OF ACTIONS

The standard rule is that the statutory period of limitation commences at the point in time at which the cause of action "accrues". Accrual is defined by statute and is generally said to occur when the allegedly negligent act occurs, or when it results in damage. For example, some jurisdictions specify the date of the alleged occurrence, holding that the cause of action accrues on the date of the alleged malpractice act. See *Payton v. Benson* (S.D.Ind. 1989). Other jurisdictions have held that an action accrues when actual damage results. See *Paul v. Skemp* (Wis. 2001) (Statute of limitations triggered by injurious result not by misdiagnosis). In *Mastro v. Brodie* (Colo.1984), the Colorado Supreme Court held that even the word "injury" is subject to different interpretations. For example, it can refer to the negligent act or omission, or to the actual physical damage that results or to the alleged injury.

Statutes of limitations may also be modified by other legislation, particularly statutes enacted specifically to address the particular concerns associated with the medical malpractice crisis. For example, in Indiana, the two year statute of limitations is "tolled" by the filing of a timely complaint with the Department of Insurance that reviews such cases and produces a written opinion. Pursuant to that legislative tolling provision, the plaintiff has a minimum of 90 days after the decision of the medical panel to file suit, and longer if the two year statute of limitations has not yet expired.

Statutes that are interpreted as defining accrual from the time of the act or omission may raise certain constitutional issues. In *Chaffin v. Nicosia* (Ind.1974), the plaintiff allegedly lost an eye at birth as a result of the use of forceps during delivery. He brought suit when he was 22 years old. In ruling on the statute of limitations issue, the court was forced to reconcile two statutes with seemingly inconsistent provisions. The statute applicable to malpractice actions required the plaintiff to bring suit within two years of the alleged incident. A second statute, applicable to lawsuits brought on behalf of the minors, allowed suit to be brought up to two years after the plaintiff attained majority. The plaintiff contended that his cause of action was not barred by the malpractice statute of limitations because he was protected by the statute which recognized the legal disability of a minor for bringing suit. Under this law, the suit was timely since it was filed less two years after the time the plaintiff reached the age of 21. The lower courts held the suit barred by the state's two-year malpractice statute. The Supreme Court reversed, holding that to bar such a claim would offend the constitution and the legislature's intent in making the disability exception. As stated by the court,

"[t]o construe [the] medical malpractice statute, which bars all suits which are not brought within two years of the occurrence of which complaint is made, as a legislative bar in all malpractice actions under all circumstances unless commenced within two years of the act complained of, discoverable or otherwise, would raise substantial questions under constitutional article relating to the guarantee of open courts and redress for injury to every man, not to mention the offense to lay concepts of justice."

Statutes of limitations, while seemingly rigid, have been subject to varying interpretations, as well as a major exception found primarily in medical malpractice actions: the discovery rule.

B.   DISCOVERY RULES:
PURE AND HYBRID

In medical malpractice cases, where expert opinion is often needed to determine that malpractice has indeed occurred, it often happens that an injured plaintiff is unaware that he has suffered an injury, particularly one that is latent. An injured patient may also not be able to reasonably associate the injury with an act or omission of the medical professional. Yet, these determinations must be made in a timely manner in order to file a claim within the traditional statute of limitations. In recognition of the reality that some medical injuries are inherently unknowable during the applicable statute of limitations, virtually all jurisdictions have carved out exceptions to the standard rule, or have redefined the statute to encompass what is known as the "discovery rule". The "discovery rule" generally provides that a cause of action must be brought within a specified period of time from the date that the injury is discovered or, in the exercise of reasonable diligence, should have been discovered. See *Burns v. Hartford Hospital* (Conn.1984) (Act specifies discovery rule); *Doyle v. Shubs* (D.Mass. 1989) (defining accrual by time of discovery of injury); *Caravaggio v. D'Agostini* (N.J.2001) (Accrual clock does not start ticking until plaintiff has evidence that reveals third party's involvement in the injury); McGraw v. United States (9th Cir.2002) (Accrual time measured starting when plaintiff learns of pre-existing condition). Pure discovery rules will allow a claim to be brought for an indefinite period of time as long as the injury has not been discovered or reasonably should not have been discovered.

An alternative or "hybrid" version of the discovery rule is followed in some states. According to the hybrid version, discovery of the injury triggers the running of the statute of limitation, but an ultimate cap or limit is placed upon the time within which discovery must occur. For example, a statute may require that an action be commenced within two years of discovery of the injury, but also contains an additional provision that requires the filing of the action within three years of the act or omission.

The latter provision is called a "statute of repose." In such a case, the claimant has at least two years to file the claim, and no more than three, depending upon when and if the injury is discovered. See *Mastro v. Brodie* (Colo.1984).

Many jurisdictions have expressly interpreted the discovery rule to apply only to situations where the injury is inherently unknowable, or to malpractice actions where a foreign body, such as a sponge, had been left in a wound during surgery. See *Cloutier v. Dalkon Shield Claimants Trust* (D.Me.1993). In a move to expand the rule, one court stated,

> "a steadily growing and now predominant line of decisions in other states which recognize the discovery rule, as such, acknowledges there is no just basis for distinguishing between different kinds of malpractice claims in applying the discovery rule, since, in all, the basic hardship and injustice of denying an injured plaintiff his day in court remains."

Moran v. Napolitano (N.J.1976). According to this line of reasoning, the discovery rule can be applied in all types of malpractice actions, including alleged error in diagnosis.

It is important to note that reliance upon a physician's assurance that an injury is not permanent may not be effective in tolling the applicable statute of limitations. In *Burns v. Hartford Hospital* (Conn. 1984), a child's leg was permanently injured from an infection resulting from contaminated intravenous tubes which were placed in the leg by the hospital staff. The doctor had assured the mother that the leg would heal completely, but the child suffered damage from scarring and an abnormality in his gait. The court held that "the act of this intervening third party, who may have misled the plaintiff about the injury's seriousness or even compounded the harm by failing to render effective treatment, cannot extend the hospital's liability beyond the statutory limitation period." The court implied, however, that there may have been a different result if the doctor had been alleged to be the agent of the hospital.

The discovery rule may also generate some confusion as to when discovery of "the injury" occurs since what constitutes the "injury" may have varying interpretations. According to Mastro, a majority of states have adopted a "legal injury" interpretation of the word "injury". Under that concept, "the statute of limitations begins to run when the claimant has knowledge of facts which would put a reasonable person on notice of the nature and extent of an injury and that the injury was caused by the wrongful conduct of another." See *Mastro*. Under that interpretation, lack of either knowledge of the injury or its possible cause would enable a plaintiff to take advantage of the discovery rule.

The question of when a patient, through the exercise of due diligence, should reasonably have discovered an injury is also the subject of frequent litigation. In *Mastro*, the plaintiff developed a discomforting keloid scar following surgery. She returned to the surgeon who provided some care and reassurance. Finally, more than two years after the surgery, the patient visited a specialist who advised her of her high risk status for keloid scarring. She filed suit. One issue before the court was whether she should have known or diligently discovered that the surgery was performed negligently. Another issue was whether the doctor failed to obtain proper informed consent, which would include information about her high risk status. The patient argued that discovery occurred upon her consultation with a specialist. The court denied summary judgment, holding that the determination of the point of discovery was a question of fact for the jury.

C. THE CONTINUING TREATMENT RULE AND FRAUDULENT CONCEALMENT

Another issue that arises in determining the time of injury for statute of limitations purposes is that treatment sometimes continues for a period of time and it can be difficult to ascertain when the negligence occurred. A number of jurisdictions have adopted a "continuing treatment" rule to address the issue. Pursuant to this doctrine, accrual of the cause of action may be tolled if there is continued treatment of the patient by the allegedly negligent physician for the particular condition that is the subject of the complaint. See *Williams v. Young* (Ga.App.2000) On appeal, the Georgia Supreme Court determined that the continuous treatment doctrine would infringe upon the legislative function in prescribing statutes of limitation. (When an illness or injury should have been diagnosed the statute of limitations is tolled until the negligent care is terminated). This rule provides an exception to the usual inflexible application of the statute of limitations and may extend the time allowed for the filing of a complaint. According to the continuing treatment rule, the cause of action would only accrue when treatment of the condition ceases. Cessation of treatment can be determined on the basis of whether a physician-patient relationship continues to exist, whether the physician continues to see the patient or whether there is additional treatment for the same condition still to be done by the physician. See *Noland v. Freeman* (Minn.1984). Whether ongoing treatment qualifies under the continuing treatment rule is a question or fact for the jury.

Finally, sometimes statutes of limitations will also be tolled if the physician is found to have "knowingly concealed" the negligent act or omission. If knowing concealment is found, a plaintiff has the statutory period of time to file the complaint which begins when he "should have known" about the negligent act or omission. See *Mastro v. Brodie* (Colo.1984). The rules for fraudulent concealment evolved through recognition of the fiduciary nature of the physician-patient relationship, which requires the physician to disclose to the patient all information that is material to his treatment. This doctrine is considered to be a form of equitable estoppel rather that an exception to the rules governing statutes of limitations.

D. REFORMS

The above mechanisms for tolling statutes of limitations evolved primarily as a result of the complexities of medical practice that may make it unfair to impose the rigid requirements of the traditional statutes of limitations. As a result a number of jurisdictions have also undertaken to reform such statutes, while still recognizing the need for imposing a limitations period. Reform of an individual statute depends upon the purpose of the statute (whether it is thought to protect primarily plaintiffs or defendants) and whether the goal is to reduce the costs of malpractice. Often the period in which a medical malpractice claim can be brought depends upon when malpractice was "discovered" and thus the claim reasonably accrued. A number of reform measures have been initiated to provide clarification of how these events are determined including the factors to be considered. The goal is to provide more predictability for defendants and their insurers, who not only defend such cases, but also set rates for insurance coverage. Statutes of repose, for example, have been enacted in recent years to limit the uncertainty of liability generated by the discovery rule.

II. GOOD SAMARITAN LAWS

Good Samaritan Laws have been enacted in most jurisdictions to induce physicians and others to render emergency care under circumstances in which they have no legal obligation to act. This includes medical emergencies that occur in areas outside of the health care setting, (e.g. on the street, in a restaurant, etc.) or inside a health care facility at a time or place that the responsible physician is not available. A physician who happens to be present or readily available can usually act in such an emergency without incurring liability even if he is negligent. Prior to enactment of Good Samaritan legislation, the common law provided a remedy by reducing the standard of care that would be used in evaluating the quality of treatment. This, however, did not discourage the initiation of malpractice actions. The Good Samaritan laws, first enacted in California, were designed to alter the common law by providing added protection for those offering services in emergency situations. Today, many laws specify guidelines where claims of ordinary negligence may be dismissed before reaching the jury. See *Colby v. Schwartz* (Cal.App.1978).

The first issue in determining whether a physician or other health care provider is covered under a particular Good Samaritan law is whether the law was intended to reach his actions under the specific circumstances. For example, the law does not apply to a physician who renders care in the normal course of his practice, such as when he is a member of an emergency room team. See *Velazquez v. Jiminez* (N.J.2002) (Physician who worked in the Maternal Fetal Care Unit and specialized in high risk patients was not protected by the Good Samaritan Act when her negligence contributed to the brain damage and eventual death of a child). On the other hand, the Good Samaritan laws have been held to apply in certain other hospital emergency situations. In *McKenna v. Cedars of Lebanon Hospital* (Cal.App.1979), where a chief resident responded to an emergency situation involving a hospital patient having post-operative seizures, the court held he was protected by the Good Samaritan law. According to *McKenna*, the applicability of the law depends on whether the doctor had a duty to respond. In that case, the hospital patient was not the resident's patient, nor did his contract with the hospital require him to respond to such emergencies.

The applicability of Good Samaritan laws varies among jurisdictions. A contrary result would be reached in a jurisdiction which precludes the application of the Good Samaritan laws in the hospital setting. For example, some statutes specify that the emergency must occur outside the physician's normal place of practice. See *McKenna*. Other statutes apply not only to physicians, but also to nurses and certain other personnel such as emergency medical technicians (EMT's) who render aid during the emergency situation. See *Chase v. Mayor and City Council of Baltimore* (Md.1999).

Other limitations which affect the application of the law depend upon specific provisions of the statute. In *Villamil v. Benages* (Ill.App.1993), the statute set forth a three-part test: (1) Care must be provided by a physician with no notice of the illness or injury; (2) emergency care must be provided; and

(3) the physician must not charge a fee. These conditions can be satisfied in the hospital setting as well as in a roadside emergency. In *Villamil,* a physician was present in the hospital attending another patient, and was called to assist in the delivery of a premature baby. The patient came into the emergency room. She did not have time to reach the hospital of her choice. On summary judgment, the physician was held to be protected by the Illinois Good Samaritan law. Utilizing the three-prong *Villamil* test, the Illinois appeals court held that an attending physician's intent to be paid for a follow up visit did not prevent the physician from raising the Good Samaritan Act as an affirmative defense. *Rivera v. Arana* (Ill.App.2001).

Other jurisdictions provide that a physician or other health professional is protected if he acts *in good faith* to render emergency care. The issue of whether the situation constitutes an emergency is sometimes resolved by an objective test, such as whether the circumstances are so pressing as to require some action to be taken. On the other hand, the requirement that there be a "good faith" belief on the part of the responding physician that an emergency exists may be a subjective determination. As a result, it may be difficult to resolve these cases by summary judgment. *Bryant v. Bakshandeh* (Cal.App.1991).

In *Bryant*, an infant boy was being prepared for elective surgery requiring insertion of a urethral catheter. The attending physician had difficulty inserting the catheter and called for the assistance of a urologist. The child later died from an infection resulting from the perforation of his rectal pouch during this preoperative procedure. A question of fact existed as to the nature of the situation and whether "in good faith" it could be perceived as an emergency. The surgeon characterized the situation as an "unforeseen complexity" which the court held was not determinative. Summary judgment was thus denied.

The varying forms of Good Samaritan legislation represent the efforts of each jurisdiction to balance two competing interests: compensating those injured through medical negligence and encouraging physicians and other health professionals to provide emergency medical care under circumstances where there is otherwise no compulsion to do so. The latter interest is promoted by Good Samaritan legislation. See *Colby v. Schwartz*.

III. OTHER AFFIRMATIVE DEFENSES

A. CONTRIBUTORY NEGLIGENCE

The traditional doctrine of contributory negligence requires that a plaintiff be free of any fault or negligence which may contribute to the severity of his injury in order to recover damages. In some jurisdictions, contributory negligence operates as a total bar to recovery. In such cases, a plaintiff who contributes to his own injury is precluded from recovering for his injuries from the tortfeasor. See *Schneider v. Revici* (2d Cir.1987). In other jurisdictions, contributory negligence is not a total bar to recovery, but instead operates to reduce plaintiff's damages by the percentage of fault attributed to his own conduct. See Comparative Negligence, below. Thus a plaintiff who is held to be 25% contributorily negligent will have his ultimate award reduce by 25%.

Contributory negligence is applicable to an action where "a party knows or by the exercise of ordinary care should have known a particular fact or circumstance and should have acted upon the fact or circumstance with reasonable care for his own safety." *Weil v. Seltzer* (D.C.Cir.1989) In the context of medical malpractice, a patient is not ordinarily expected to know that a prescribed treatment or procedure was performed negligently, or that there were undisclosed risks that may have influenced his decision to undergo the procedure. Such medical decisions often require the expertise of the physician. As a consequence, contributory negligence is generally not available to mitigate a physician's negligence if the patient was merely following the orders of the physician. *Weil v. Seltzer*.

Similarly, a patient is not necessarily contributorily negligent if he seeks consultation from another doctor during the course of treatment, and thereafter declines to follow the consulting physician's advise. Here, the original physician-patient relationship was not terminated, and the patient does not contribute to his own injury in following the advise of the treating physician. See *Weinstock v. Ott* (Ind. App.1983). In *Ott*, a woman, suffering from abdominal pain for almost two years, was under the care of a physician when she sought the advice of a second physician. She had already undergone multiple tests during two hospitalizations. The consulting physician recommended more tests, although he was not able to provide the patient with any other diagnosis at that point. The woman declined to undergo the additional testing but continued to see her original physician. In fact, she checked herself out of the second hospital, after many tests failed to provide any explanation or yield any improvement of her condition. Nearly four years later, the condition was finally correctly diagnosed at the second hospital. Nevertheless, the patient eventually died of complications brought about by the advanced stage of the disease. The court held that she was not contributorily negligent as a matter of law in failing to follow the advise of the consultant or by checking herself out of the second hospital. She had been provided with no further information, and thus opted to continue to see and follow the advise of her original physician for the entire period of time.

B.   COMPARATIVE NEGLIGENCE

Comparative negligence is a related doctrine also devised to reduce the compensation to a plaintiff who, in some way contributes to his own injury. There are several forms of comparative negligence, and many jurisdictions have adopted one form or another. In general, the theory of comparative negligence is that any negligence on the part of the plaintiff is "compared" to that of the tortfeasor, and any damages ultimately awarded to the plaintiff are reduced by the percentage of negligence attributed to the plaintiff.

There are three possible forms of comparative negligence adopted in various jurisdictions. The first is "pure" comparative negligence. In such a case a plaintiff, regardless of how much his own negligence contributes to his injury, will still be able to recover something from a negligent tortfeasor. The percentage of negligence attributed to his conduct is deducted in the same percentage from the dollar amount of the total award. See *Shelton v. United States* (E.D.Mo.1992). The remaining forms of comparative negligence also permit recovery of a comparatively negligent plaintiff to be reduced by the percentage attributed to his own negligence. However, they only operate when the plaintiff's contribution is less that 50 or 51 percent of the total negligence (depending upon statute.) This is similar to, and an alternative to, contributory negligence statutes.

Comparative negligence attempts to apportion fault and damages based on the relative contribution to the injury by all the parties involved. The respective contributions toward causation may be compared and the damages due to the patient may be reduced in proportion to the fault of the patient. In *Shelton*, the court held that the physician was negligent in not prescribing antibiotics for a patient's bite wound. However, the patient's negligence in not following discharge instructions and returning promptly for medical care when infection was observed was held to constitute a 50 percent contribution to the injury, resulting in subsequent amputation of the finger. Pursuant to the applicable statute, plaintiff's award of damages was reduced by 50 percent. Physicians may prove comparative negligence against subsequent physicians. See *Marina Emergency Medical Group v. Superior Ct. of Los Angles County* (Cal.App.2000). In *Marina*, the defendant doctor performed emergency medical treatment on the plaintiff's thumb. Following the emergency treatment, the plaintiff visited his general physician who, one month later referred the plaintiff to a surgeon. By this time, the plaintiff's thumb had suffered irreparable harm. The court held that the defendant was entitled to have the damages equitably divided between the negligent physicians.

C. AVOIDABLE CONSEQUENCES AND LAST CLEAR CHANCE

The theory of comparative negligence is often used to apportion damage when the related doctrines of "avoidable consequences" or "last clear chance" are set forth. Each is based upon the assumption that in some cases a plaintiff, while not responsible for his injury, had some opportunity to avoid or mitigate the results. These doctrines operate after the legal wrong has caused the harm. The theory is that the patient should not recover for what he could have avoided or mitigated, although recovery need not be totally barred. Contributory negligence, in contrast, can operate before or concurrently with the medical malpractice and may bar a plaintiff's recovery. See *Ostrowski v. Azzara* (N.J. 1988).

Comparative negligence may still be applied even in situations where the injured plaintiff relocates to another jurisdiction and continues care in that location. For example, a federal district court in New Jersey held that such relocation did not prevent the allocation of causative fault between the non-settling physicians and the settling physician in another jurisdiction, since the claims were found to be identical and interwoven. See *Carter v. University of Medicine and Dentistry of New Jersey—Rutgers Medical School* (D.N.J.1994). Conflict of laws rules may also affect the application of contributory or comparative negligence law when a plaintiff moves to another jurisdiction.

D. PRIOR AND SUBSEQUENT TORTFEASORS

A physician who treats a patient and thereby incurs a professional duty may also be held liable for injuries caused by a subsequent physician, if such subsequent physician attempts to remedy a condition caused by him. See *Daly v. United States* (9th Cir.1991). Thus a physician who causes injury may be held liable for subsequent aggravation of that injury even if it occurs through additional medical malpractice. See *Moller v. North Shore University Hospital* (E.D.N.Y.1992); *Tyler v. Ahmed* (11th Cir.1987).

Many states have adopted some form of the Uniform Contribution Among Tortfeasors Act which would provide a right of contribution among joint tortfeasors. Ordinarily a joint tortfeasor is not entitled to receive money from contributing tortfeasors unless he has fully paid the common liability or paid more that his pro rata share. See Fed. R. Civ. P., Rule 14 Annotations; *Smith v. Whitmore* (3d Cir. 1959); *Huggins v. Graves* (E.D.Tenn. 1962); Penn. Uniform Contribution Among Joint Tortfeasors Act, 12 P.S. sec. 2083.

E.　ASSUMPTION OF THE RISK

"Assumption of the Risk" is a legal doctrine based upon the premise that some products or procedures contain inherent risks. The law holds that when a patient is informed of these risks, and he chooses to proceed nevertheless, he may assume responsibility for adverse occurrences that result. Assumption of the risk, as compared to contributory or comparative negligence, focuses on what the patient actually knew as opposed to what the patient should have known. For example, if a patient knew that a particular risk was associated with a medical procedure and nevertheless submitted to it, assumption of the risk may bar recovery for any resulting injuries associated with that known risk, although not for a physician's negligence. See *Weil v. Seltzer* (D.C.Cir.1989).

At common law, one could not assume the risk of another's negligence. Such an action would rarely be sustained, even if the individual did purport to assume the risk of another's negligence. See Exculpatory Clauses, infra. In *Schneider v. Revici* (2d Cir.1987), the second circuit held that a patient who consented to non-conventional experimental treatment, foregoing traditional methods, might be held to have assumed the risk of any worsening of his condition. The use of non-traditional therapies, unless negligently selected, would probably constitute an inherent risk.

Assumption of the risk can either be express (as through a consent form) or implied by the circumstances. In order for a patient to be held to expressly assume a risk, there must be clear evidence, such as a properly executed consent form. To claim express assumption of the risk as a defense, there must be evidence that the patient had knowledge of the risk, appreciated and understood the nature of the risk, and voluntarily chose to incur it. See *Shorter v. Drury* (Wash.1985). *Shorter* involved a Jehovah's Witness who was advised of the need for a blood transfusion but declined, instead executing a written "Refusal to Permit a Blood Transfusion." A Release of liability was also executed to address any consequences associated with declining the transfusion. The patient was admitted to the hospital for a dilation and curettage procedure and subsequently bled to death after the surgeon negligently lacerated her uterus. The court held that the release did not exculpate the physician from his negligence in lacerating the patient's uterus. It did, however, constitute an assumption of the risk of refusing blood. The patient's death would otherwise have been avoided by the transfusion. The court held that the physician could still be liable for his negligence, although damages were reduced by the patient's assumption of the risk.

IV. LIMITATIONS ON LIABILITY

A. RELEASES

At common law, a release of one joint tortfeasor released all tortfeasors from liability. This rule evolved from the principle that a victim was entitled to be compensated only once for his injury and thus would avoid unjust enrichment. This rule applied to concurrent tortfeasors as well as those acting in concert. The common law rule seems to have developed as a result of confusion within some courts about the concepts of "satisfaction" and "release". Satisfaction indicates full compensation for the injury, while a release is a surrender of the cause of action, whether or not it has been satisfied. Many courts hold that a release of one of concurrent tortfeasors releases all the others, without considering whether there has been just or adequate compensation. For example, in *Tyler v. Ahmed* (11th Cir.1987), the court held that a plaintiff who settled a claim with her auto insurance company for all of her injuries cannot thereafter bring a malpractice action against the physician who treated her injuries. An express settlement of all damages to the plaintiff usually results in the rights of the insured being subrogated to those of the insurance company. The court also pointed out that the insured knowingly compromised all of her claims as part of the settlement, regardless of whether she believes that she was fully compensated.

The modern view of releases is that, absent clear language to the contrary, a subsequent tortfeasor such as a negligent treating physician is *not* released from liability as a matter of law. The common law interpretation of releases has been modified by statute in many jurisdictions. For example, in those jurisdictions that have adopted the "Uniform Contribution Among Tortfeasors Act", a tortfeasor would only be released from liability *"if the release so provides"*.

In *Morgan v. Cohen* (Md.1987), a malpractice action was brought against a physician for negligent treatment of injuries that the plaintiff sustained in an auto accident. The claim had been settled with the auto insurance company and the settlement included a general release. In contrast to *Tyler, Morgan* held that because Maryland had abrogated the common law rule by adopting the Uniform Contribution Among Tortfeasors Act, the general release did not discharge the physician as a matter of law. The determination of whether the physician was released was held to depend upon the intent of the parties and whether the satisfaction included all the damages. *Morgan*, supra.

In *Douglas v. U.S. Tobacco Company* (8th Cir. 1982), the eight circuit interpreted the phrase "all other persons" contained in a general release to satisfy the "if the release so provides" condition in the local version of the Uniform Contribution Among Tortfeasors Act. Thus, any subsequent tortfeasor would be discharged from liability regardless of actual compensation that might have been received. This position is followed by a majority of jurisdictions.

Similarly, a South Dakota court held that a general release, using the terms "doctors... and all other persons", signed as part of a medical malpractice action, barred a claim against a pharmaceutical company in a subsequent products liability, fraud and misrepresentation action. *Enos v. Key Pharmaceuticals, Inc.* (8th Cir. 1997) The court found that the previously signed document "released all entities from all claims of every kind, *including, but not limited to* claims resulting from negligence and malpractice". *See Flynn v. Lockhart* (S.D.1995); *Cleland v. United States,* (8th Cir.1989). The court in *Enos* stated that it is the intent of the parties that controls, as evidenced by the language of the release.

A written release that is silent about its effect upon subsequent litigants may be interpreted differently. *McCullough v. Bethany Medical Center* (Kan. 1984) was such a case in which the court held that such parties were presumed not released. Furthermore, parol evidence was permitted to determine the intention of the parties. Likewise, certain statutory provisions may require that the release expressly release subsequent tortfeasors in order for them to avoid liability. See *Moller v. North Shore*

University Hospital (E.D.N.Y.1992). There the applicable statute also provided that subsequent claims would be set-off by the amount of damages already received.

B.   EXCULPATORY CLAUSES

Occasionally a physician or institution will attempt to make an agreement with a patient that exempts the health care provider from liability for ordinary negligence. For example, some clinics which train students have attempted to offer services at a reduced price in consideration of absolving the provider of liability. See *Emory University v. Porubiansky* (Ga.1981). Exculpatory clauses in agreements which limit liability for negligence are uniformly held to be unenforceable for purposes of medical malpractice as contrary to public policy. See *Tunkl v. Regents of the University of California* (Cal.1963). In *Tunkl*, a charitable research hospital required patients, as a condition of admission, to release the hospital for the negligence of its employees, as long as it used due care in selecting them. The applicable California Civil Code prohibited exculpatory clauses for "violations of law, whether willful or negligent", which affect the public interest. The court commented that the rule against exculpatory clauses might be different in the case where a private transaction had no effect on the public interest.

Where a patient enters a hospital, particularly a charitable research hospital, the public interest is clear. While definitions of public interest may vary, *Tunkl* outlined several factors which would tend to affect its characterization: (1) the business involved is generally considered suitable for public regulation, or the service is of great importance or necessity to the general public; (2) the party seeking the exculpatory clause has held itself out as willing to serve any or all of the public; (3) the party is often of superior bargaining strength, given the nature of the service; (4) an adhesion type contract is offered with the exculpatory clause; and (5) the person or property is under the control of the party promoting the clause. If a contract meets some or all of this criteria, an exculpatory clause regarding medical malpractice is likely to be held invalid.

C.   ARBITRATION PROVISIONS

Arbitration provisions, in contrast to exculpatory clauses, address the method through which compensation of an injury will be determined. They do not attempt to avoid liability. Agreements to arbitrate may be made privately between the parties or pursuant to legislation. In either case, these agreements generally constitute a viable alternative to litigation. Consideration may be given to whether or not they constitute terms of adhesion. In *Morris v. Metriyakool* (Mich.1984), upon admission to the hospital, a patient was offered, within the admission form, an option that any dispute arising out of her medical care would be submitted to arbitration. Michigan's Medical Malpractice Arbitration Act permitted such a provision. The court held that as long as the statutory procedures were followed, the Act did not violate due process and therefore was not unconstitutional.

Michigan's Medical Malpractice Arbitration Act is representative of a number of recent statutory schemes designed to deal with the litigation crisis that has resulted from large numbers of malpractice actions. The Michigan act requires that submission to arbitration must be voluntary in that an agreement which contains such a provision must (a) highlight the arbitration clause, (b) make it optional and (c) make it revocable within some limited period of time. If arbitration is accepted, the composition of the tribunal must be fair, and basic requirements of due process must be met. See *Morris*.

V. IMMUNITIES

Through tradition and common law, medical institutions and certain of their personnel were once afforded either absolute or qualified immunity from liability for acts of negligence. The immunity was based upon the nature and position of the institution, the source of its funding and available sources of malpractice insurance. The policy reasons promoting immunity typically reflected the need to protect hospitals or medical personnel who provide necessary (and even gratuitous) medical care from the burdens of tort claims and expensive insurance policies. Immunities developed from concern that the cost of liability would divert the institution's funds from provision of medical care. Immunity was afforded to charitable institutions and governmental entities, both at the state and federal level. Some immunities continue to exist today, but the original intent of the legislation has long passed.

A. CHARITABLE IMMUNITY

Historically, the doctrine of charitable immunity applied to non-profit charitable institutions—the typical classification of most hospitals. This immunity from tort claims was provided in recognition of their limited sources of funding, and in consideration of their efforts to provide medical care for all regardless of ability to pay. As hospitals evolved from charitable institutions to multi-million dollar corporate entities, the need for charitable immunity slowly eroded. The need to encourage medical care to be provided according to standards of due care, along with a recognition that injured parties should not be required to remain uncompensated, slowly caused the doctrine of charitable immunity to be abrogated in varying degrees in all but a handful of jurisdictions.

Total abrogation of charitable immunity has occurred in 27 states, including California, New York and Washington. Other states have limited liability to a certain dollar amount, or in accordance with the hospital's liability insurance. Massachusetts, for example, limits the liability of its hospitals and other charitable organizations to $20,000 per occurrence, thus retaining charitable immunity beyond that extent. New Jersey limits the liability of charitable organizations to $10,000. The total or partial abrogation of the charitable immunity doctrine reflects a legislative effort to balance the competing interests of the injured party and the medical institution. For example, in *Peters v. McCalla* (D.S.C. 1978), the court stated that

"[o]ne would have to ignore the realities of business and commerce to suggest that these reasonable rates (of insurance) will not skyrocket with the fall of the doctrine of charitable immunity. There is no better example of what the hospitals in this state can expect to occur in regard to their insurance rates than the tremendous rise in cost of medical malpractice for doctors over the past several years in response to the increased number of malpractice claims brought in the courts of this state."

Consequently, South Carolina abrogated charitable immunity in such cases that an injured patient could show a reckless disregard of the patient's rights. Similarly, other states have abrogated immunity only in cases of wanton or willful misconduct, or gross negligence. See *Seiderman v. American Institute for Mental Studies* (D.N.J.1987).

Seiderman also demonstrated that a jurisdiction can apply charitable immunity doctrine to an institution in another state. *Seiderman* held that New Jersey's charitable immunity doctrine applied to an out-of-state charitable, non-profit institution, *which had contact* with New Jersey by conducting non-profit activities within the state. The doctrine was held to bar a claim by a New Jersey resident against the out-of-state hospital.

Massachusetts, on the other hand, recently reaffirmed its commitment to charitable immunity. Vacating a lower court's award of damages in excess of the state's statutory immunity cap, the Supreme

Judicial Court held that even where the defendant hospital had failed to produce records that were essential to the plaintiff's case, the court could not abrogate its immunity as a discovery sanction without legislative approval. Keene v. Brigham's Women's Hospital (Mass.2003).

B. GOVERNMENTAL IMMUNITY

Like charitable immunity, governmental immunity limits the liability of certain institutions (including hospitals) which are associated with the state or federal government. The immunity afforded such state and federal institutions flows from the Eleventh Amendment's prohibition of an individual's right to bring a private claim against the state. Like charitable immunity, governmental immunity has also seen substantial erosion in modern times. This is significant in light of the number of governmental facilities providing medical care. In 1946 the federal government enacted the Federal Torts Claim Act through which it abrogates its own immunity (to the extent of $100,000) and thus consents to be sued for most torts, including medical malpractice. Recovery cannot exceed $100,000.

Government immunity at the state level varies among jurisdictions. An example of state level governmental immunity is highlighted in *Tobias v. Phelps* (Mich.App.1985). Michigan's governmental immunity provision encompasses defendants who, in good faith, act in the course or their employment or authority, or reasonably believe they so act, and who perform "discretionary (state) tasks". See *Patten v. Commonwealth* (Va.2001) (Commonwealth entitled to liability immunity because state hospital employees negligent acts were discretionary tasks). Difficulty arises, however, in determining which functions are considered "discretionary" as opposed to those that are considered "ministerial". Governmental immunity is only granted when the tortfeasor performs a discretionary function. The rule of thumb seems to be that decisions about what medical care is needed is considered "discretionary", while the act of actually carrying out such decisions is considered "ministerial". Accordingly, *Tobias* held that a state hospital may be liable for the death of a patient in a mental health facility who died from an asthma attack while confined to a "quiet room", if confining the patient to the room was considered a ministerial function. The hospital would not be protected by governmental immunity if the jury found that it was not a discretionary decision that caused the death of the patient.

C. STATUTORY IMMUNITY

In some circumstances more that one set of legislation might affect the liability of certain governmental employees. For example, members of the military, and even many federal employees, are often precluded from bringing tort actions against the government for service-related injuries. See 1 L. Jayson, Handling Federal Tort Claims, secs. 153–155 (1985). In lieu of seeking tort claims, most military and federal employees are entitled to various administrative benefits for personal injuries.

The context in which statutory immunity arises most frequently is suits by military employees against doctors or psychiatrists affiliated with a Veteran's Hospital. The policy reasons justifying immunity of military personnel include the consideration that such doctors must also respond to military orders in providing medical care. See *Baker v. Barber* (6th Cir.1982). In *Baker*, two statutory provisions were triggered when a civilian employee attempted to bring suit against army physicians for negligent treatment of a work related injury. The Federal Employee Compensation Act (FECA) precludes relief under the Federal Torts Claim Act (FTCA) for tort claims, including those alleging medical malpractice. The Military Medical Malpractice Statute grants immunity to military physicians, requiring the plaintiff to rely on the FTCA. Recognizing that statutory immunity barred all suits, the court pointed out that the employee nevertheless would be compensated under FECA.

CHAPTER SEVEN

VICARIOUS LIABILITY AND MULTIPLE DEFENDANTS

I. IN GENERAL: VICARIOUS TORT LIABILITY

Vicarious liability generally arises from the master-servant or principal-agent relationship created through employment or contract. The doctrine holds that a principal may be held liable for the tortious acts of its employees or agents if they acted within the scope of their employment or agency relationship. See generally *Ward v. Gordon* (9th Cir.1993). Other circumstances such as the formation of a partnership or a professional corporation may also subject the principals to vicarious liability.

In the medical field where many licensed independent practitioners function as independent contractors, the question of whether an agency relationship exists becomes a critical determination for purposes of vicarious liability. The finding of an agency relationship generally requires the presence of three distinct elements: (1) some manifestation of consent by the principal that the agent will act on his behalf; (2) acceptance of that undertaking by the agent; and (3) an understanding between the parties that the activities undertaken by the agent are

179

subject to the control of the principal. See generally *Karas v. Jackson* (E.D.Pa.1983).

Manifestation of consent by the principal can be express, as by word or written contract, or implied by the conduct or inaction of the principal. Once the agency relationship is established, the next inquiry is whether the alleged the negligent act of the agent was within the scope of the agency relationship. Such a finding generally requires the following: (1) that the conduct be of the kind that the agent or employee was expected to perform; (2) that the act have occurred substantially within the authorized space and time limits; and (3) that there be involved to some degree an intent to serve the master. See Alfred F. Conrad et al., Enterprise Organizations, sec. 2 (4th ed. 1987). Whether the allegedly negligent activity is within the scope of employment is often determined in part by the codes of professional conduct and provider policies.

Vicarious liability is generally found in employment situations, and is the basis for such doctrines as the so-called "borrowed servants" and "captain of the ship" as well as respondeat superior, infra. In all of these relationships, the actor is primarily responsible for his own negligence. If a principal is vicariously liable, one of two situations is likely to result: either the employee or agent will seek indemnification from the principal, or the original action will name multiple defendants who will sort out liability if and when a judgment is rendered against them.

A. THE "BORROWED SERVANT" RULE

One basis for the "borrowed servant" rule, a special rule of agency which holds principals liable for the negligence of their agents under the doctrine of respondeat superior, is the Restatement (Agency) 2d sec. 227. According to the Restatement, a servant in the general employ of one master or principal (e.g. the hospital) can be also in the special employ of another (e.g. a specific staff physician) for a particular purpose. In those cases in which the doctrine applies, the master, whose business purpose is forwarded by the loaned servant, will be responsible for any tortious acts committed within the scope of the agency. Under certain circumstances, the physician who borrows the servant may also be responsible for his negligence.

The borrowed servant doctrine, however, is not without limits, even in those jurisdictions which recognize it. In *Ferguson v. Dyer* (Ohio App.2002), the treating physician entered a standing order to monitor his patient upon the patient being removed from a ventilator. Due to a nurse's negligent monitoring and untimely notification of the on-call physician that the patient's condition had deteriorated, there was a delay in re-intubation, and the patient suffered serious brain damage and permanent mental deficits. The nurse in *Ferguson* was held not to be a loaned servant of the treating physician because the physician did not exercise control over the detail and manner in which the nurse carried out her orders, the physician had no control over the nursing assignments, and the advisability of the standing order to monitor was not being called into question.

Whether there exists a "right of control" generally determines whether the servant has been "borrowed" by a temporary, second master. In *Sparger v. Worley Hospital* (Tex.1977), a borrowed employee was defined as "one, who, while in the general employment of the hospital, is subject to the right of the physician to direct or control the details of the particular work inquired about, and is not merely cooperating with suggestions of said physician." In *Sparger*, an action was brought against a surgeon for injury resulting when a sponge was left in a patient's body during surgery. The nurses responsible for the sponge count were found by the jury not to be the "borrowed servants" of the surgeon. The court determined it was a jury question upon which reasonable minds could differ as to whether the surgeon "directed" the sponge count. Specific duties concerning this procedure were outlined for the nurses in the hospital procedure manual. The case was ultimately remanded to determine if the finding that the nurses were not borrowed servants was against the great weight of the evidence.

In *Rogers v. Duke* (Tex.App.1989), the court affirmed summary judgment for the physician upon similar facts, holding that the operating room nurses were not the borrowed servants of the surgeon. In *Rogers*, however, the surgeon had already left the operating room when the sponge count was done. The reviewing court relied on factors presented in *Sparger* which supported the finding that the nurses were not borrowed servants: "(1) the defendant-physician did not participate in selection of the nurses; (2) the hospital's policy and procedure manual detailed the duties of the circulating and scrub nurses, including general instructions that applied to both nurses; (3) the sponge count procedures were intended to be used without regard to which surgeon was performing an operation; (4) the defendant-physician did not direct the nurses to make a sponge count." On the basis of the above factors, and the fact that the surgeon was *not present* to supervise at the close of surgery, the court affirmed summary judgment. No jury determination was necessary to resolve the issue of whether the nurses were borrowed servants of the physician.

Two issues emerge in the analysis of the borrowed servant rule: (1) whether the physician had the right to control or actually assumed control; and (2) assuming he/she did, whether both masters can be held responsible. Courts differ in their approach to these issues.

Sparger required that the physician have only a right of control, while some other courts require that the physician have actually assumed control. Among the latter, presence of the physician when the negligence occurs is particularly significant. *Kitto v. Gilbert* (Colo.App.1977), held that a physician is liable for the acts of hospital employees assisting during the surgery where he had assumed control at the time the negligent act allegedly occurs. In

Kitto, a patient, while inadequately anesthetized, coughed. The cough resulted in the tube delivering the anesthesia to become disconnected during the preparation for surgery, and eventually in the loss of one of the patient's eyes. The court held that the surgeon could be held responsible for negligence of the hospital employees if he had assumed control of the operating room. Thus, if such control was found, the physician, rather than the hospital, would be held liable.

A Washington court also addressed the question of whether a borrowed servant was no longer within the control of his original master. See *Ward v. Gordon* (9th Cir.1993). *Ward* involved the alleged negligence of a military physician who was serving a six month residency at a private hospital. Federal law would preclude personal liability of the physician if it were found that he was acting within the scope of the government's employment. The ninth circuit affirmed the district court's finding that the physician was a borrowed servant of the private hospital. The status of borrowed servant was determined by four factors:

"(1) whether the borrowing master has the right to hire and fire the servant; (2) whether the borrowing master has the right to direct the manner in which the servant performs his duties; (3) whether the value of any equipment the servant brings with him has any bearing on the servant's continued relationship with the borrowing master; and (4) whether the borrowing master exclusively controls or has the exclusive right to control the servant."

Once again, the court held that the right to control (as opposed to actual control) was the pertinent issue.

Ward is consistent with the position of the Restatement (Agency) 2d sec. 226, which provides that it is possible for a person to be a servant of two masters if service to the new master does not involve abandonment of service to the original. In *Ward*, the physician was able to concurrently perform his duties for both the private hospital and the government. Therefore, federal law provided him with immunity from personal liability, although the United States, as the original master, could be held liable for his negligence while practicing at the private hospital.

In suits not involving protected federal employees, both masters are potentially responsible for the negligence of the servant. As explained in the Florida case of *Abraham v. United States* (11th Cir. 1991), there is a presumption that a borrowed servant remains in the general employ of his original master, as long as he still performs the master's business. In cases involving medical personnel, it is not uncommon for a single act to benefit two masters, or for liability to be incurred on behalf of both.

B.   PHYSICIAN LIABILITY UNDER RESPONDEAT SUPERIOR

Physicians who practice in hospitals are generally not employees but independent contractors. Traditionally they exercise absolute control over the course of the medical care that they provide to their patients. This right of control, particularly for surgeons using the operating room, has resulted in various rules of liability. One is an adaptation of the borrowed servant rule, supra, known as the "captain of the ship" doctrine. Under this doctrine, it is assumed that the surgeon (like the naval captain) has complete control over the operation and the medical personnel (or "crew") who assist in the surgery. Pursuant to this doctrine, the surgeon or physician, merely by virtue of his presence in the operating room, is responsible for the actions, including the negligence of all persons working "under his command". In recent years, this doctrine has either been rejected or fallen into disfavor in many jurisdictions. See *Lewis v. Physicians Ins. Co.* (Wis.2001). *Lewis* rejected the "captain of the ship" doctrine, finding that it was "an antiquated doctrine that fails to reflect the emergence of hospitals as modern health care facilities."

Respondeat Superior is a more established and accepted doctrine holding physicians liable for the negligence of those under their control. Physician liability under respondeat superior is more clearly applicable if an employee of the physician such as a nurse or technician acts negligently. Nevertheless, the physician is also potentially responsible for non-employee personnel under agency principles such as the "borrowed servant" rule. Moreover, the fact that the physician is not present when the negligent act occurs does not necessarily exonerate him from responsibility.

Karas v. Jackson (E.D.Pa.1983), provides some guidelines for determining the conditions under which liability may be imposed. Karas involved the death of a woman during what was alleged to be negligence in the performance of amniocentesis. The plaintiff-husband attempted to hold the director of the Division of Medical Genetics responsible for failing to warn his wife of the risks of the procedure, failing to exercise due care, and failing to perform the procedure in a proper and safe manner. Liability was alleged even though the director was not directly involved in patient care. *Karas*. Vicarious liability was alleged on the basis of respondeat superior, which requires the presence of an agency relationship. In order to find such a relationship, the court held that there must be both a manifestation of consent to act on the physician's behalf, and acceptance of the task by the agent. The court also held, however, that the act must be *subject to the control of the physician. Karas* refused to hold the physician-director liable for the death of the patient. Although he may have been involved in "establishing general guidelines for the recommendation or performance of the amniocentesis procedure" the court found that he was not "in charge". He did not employ the physician who performed the procedure, received no benefit from it, and did not direct the actual procedure which resulted in the patient's death.

Hunnicutt v. Wright (5th Cir.1993) also supports the notion that an agency relationship is required, including a certain degree of control. The fifth circuit reversed a district court decision holding a surgeon liable for the negligence of the scrub nurse in failing to inspect an instrument. As a result of the negligence, a screw and washer were left in the chest of the patient. The court held that although the doctor may also have been negligent, he was not liable for the acts or omissions of the nurse if she was not subject to his direction and control. Where the nature of the task (inspecting instruments) requires it to be performed out of the presence of the surgeon and does not require his "specialized medical knowledge", negligence may be imputed to the hospital, but not the surgeon. The hospital was vicariously liable for the negligence of its employee (the nurse) for acts within the scope of her employment, including the inspection of instruments. She was not, however, a borrowed servant for that purpose.

Although the presence of the physician is generally required in order for a court to find that he exercised the requisite degree of control, there are exceptions to the rule. For example, in *Walstad v. University of Minnesota Hospitals* (8th Cir.1971) the appeals court found the physician vicariously liable under principles of respondeat superior for the negligent act of a nurse in administering penicillin to a patient. The patient had a known allergy to the drug. The court imputed liability for this negligence to the physician even though he was not present when the medication was given. Liability resulted because nurses can only administer drugs upon an order of the physician, and he should have known of the allergy. Thus, the physician was held to have exerted the requisite control through the written orders left for the hospital personnel.

Notwithstanding *Walstad*, it is certainly not inevitable that physicians will be held liable for the manner in which their orders are carried out. In *Ferguson*, supra, a physician was held not liable for the delayed intubation of his patient caused by a nurse's failure to monitor the patient and notify the physician of a change in the patient's condition. This delay ultimately lead to profound brain damage and permanent mental impairment. The physician issued a standing order to monitor the patient, but he was not present to constantly monitor and assess the patient's condition. Even though the physician had given the order to monitor, he was not responsible for the nurse's negligence in monitoring the patient. The nurse was employed by the hospital, and the physician had no control over the nursing assignments. The court notes that the physician's clinical judgment as evidenced in his standing order to monitor was not in question, and physician's instructions alone did not create a master-servant relationship.

C. PHYSICIAN LIABILITY FOR OTHER PHYSICIANS

The basic principle regarding physician liability for acts of another physician is that no liability will result unless there is control over such other physician. See *Karas*. The requirement of control, which

might be present in an employment or agency relationship, is necessary for vicarious liability. For
example, in *Royer v. St. Paul Fire and Marine Ins.
Co.* (La.App.1987), the court held that a surgeon
"was not vicariously liable for alleged negligence on
the part of radiologist in performing an arteriogram
on plaintiff's decedent under principles of respondeat superior, as neither physician was agent, servant,
or employee of the other and two physicians practiced different types of medicine completely independent of each other."

When consultation with a specialist is involved in
the care of a patient, the question arises as to
whether the primary physician might be liable for
the negligence of a consultant. Often it depends
upon the particular fact situation, as well as the law
of the jurisdiction. It may also depend upon the
extent of simultaneous involvement with the patient and whether the care rendered by either physician was entirely independent of the other.

In *Largess v. Tatem* (Vt.1972), the original physician, a general practitioner, admitted a woman to
the hospital for a fracture of her left hip. After
initially treating the patient, he referred her to a
specialist in orthopedic surgery who successfully
repaired the patient's hip. After the surgery the
specialist arranged for the patient to receive physical therapy, and instructed that there be no weight
bearing on the operative hip. The surgeon then
allowed the patient's care to be resumed by the
general practitioner. When she was discharged by
the general practitioner, however, he neglected to

advise against full weight bearing on the operative hip. The result was a failure of the fixation device and a second operation to repair the damage.

In *Largess*, the general practitioner was found liable even though the surgeon had not left specific discharge instructions for the patient. Although the surgeon had permitted the general practitioner to take over the patient's post-operative care, the general practitioner should have known, on the basis of the surgeon's notes and his own expertise, that weight bearing could cause danger to the patient. Furthermore, if he was uncertain about discharge instructions, he should have consulted with the specialist. As stated by the court, "voluntary ignorance affords no protection from legal liability."

In contrast to *Largess*, the third circuit held there was no liability for the alleged negligence of a consultant. In *Suire v. Lake Charles Memorial Hospital* (La.App.1991), a neurosurgeon requested a consultation with an internist when post-operatively, his patient showed signs of a rare infection. The court found that the neurosurgeon deferred to the judgment of the internist, and therefore was not liable for any negligence that might have occurred.

Courts have held that a referring physician generally is not liable for negligence in the consulting physician's care "unless there is some control in the course of the treatment of one by the other, agency or concert of action, or negligence in the referral." "Concert of action" means that both physicians continue to treat the patient (and charge for patient visits), or that the referring physician remains present during the patient's treatment, thus retaining some control over the course of treatment provided to the patient.

Where one physician "covers" for another, i.e. treats another physician's patients on a rotating basis during vacations, weekends or other "on-call" time, there is generally no liability imposed on the regular physician for the negligence of the covering physician. In *Kavanaugh by Gonzales v. Nussbaum* (N.Y.1988), for example, the court held that an obstetrician was not vicariously liable for injury to a baby born in distress as a result of complications from an undiagnosed condition of the placenta. Although the court found that the "covering" or "on-call" arrangement was mutually beneficial, there was no agency relationship because there did not exist any element of control. The court examined the policy concerns that weighed against extending vicarious liability to the covering physician. Rotating coverage is necessary for the continual patient care around the clock. Imposing liability on a physician merely because he participates in an on-call arrangement would discourage practice in certain specialties, and tends to increase the cost of medical care, both of which are detrimental to the public interest.

Steinberg v. Dunseth (Ill.App.1994), followed the reasoning of *Kavanaugh* in declining to hold physicians liable for negligence resulting from coverage arrangements. In both, a woman died from complications resulting from an allegedly negligent surgical procedure performed by a covering surgeon. The courts refused, however, to hold the regular surgeon liable unless there was evidence of his own negligence in selecting an incompetent covering physician.

Negligent selection of a physician to work in collaboration to perform surgery may also lead to liability. For example, *Kitto v. Gilbert* (Colo.App. 1977) held the surgeon liable for the actions of the anesthesiologist whom he had selected for the procedure. But while negligence in the selection of another physician may lead to liability, it requires that the selecting physician have knowledge of the other's negligent propensities and thereafter fail to address the problem. Alternatively, if he fails to make reasonable inquiry about the competence of a physician he selects, he may also become liable for any injury caused by such other physician. The physician-patient relationship thus creates a duty not only to perform non-negligently but also to select others who would be expected to perform competently.

A number of jurisdictions would also hold a physician liable for successive acts of malpractice based on the position of the Restatement (Second) of Torts § 457 (1965). This means that a physician who performs negligently may also be liable for any injury resulting from the malpractice of a subsequent physician whose treatment was sought to repair the injury caused by the initial negligence. Liability will not be imposed on such initial physician for care which is considered to be independent of his treatment. In order to be held liable, the care of the initial physician must result in an identifiable harm which the subsequent physician's efforts were intended to address. See *Daly v. United States* (9th Cir.1991).

II. PARTNERSHIPS AND PROFESSIONAL CORPORATIONS

A. THE PARTNERSHIP

At common law the partnership was the predominant form of professional association utilized by medical practitioners. A partnership can arise without any express verbal or written agreement by the partners. A majority of jurisdictions have adopted the Uniform Partnership Act of 1914 (in its revised form) which is considered to be a "default" statute to provide guidance for issues that arise within the partnership in the absence of any agreement. See Enterprise Organizations, supra.

Where there exists a partnership arrangement, express or implied, liability of the partners is joint and several. When an individual partner is sued, he need not be the actual tortfeasor; he may be a partner of the tortfeasor who had no personal involvement at all. See *Zuckerman v. Antenucci* (N.Y.Sup.1984). As explained by one court, "on the principle of mutual agency, the partnership, or every member of a partnership, is liable for torts committed by one of the members acting in the scope of the firm business although they do not participate in, ratify or have knowledge of such torts." *Schmitz v. St. Lukes Hospital, Inc. et al.*

(D.N.D.1966). Therefore, the implication is that within this arrangement the plaintiff may bring an action against the partnership or any individual partner; it is not necessary to join all the members to ensure compensation in the event that a judgment is rendered.

At least one court has attempted to refine the concept of joint and several liability to better reflect the intent of partnership liability. The court held that a physician who was not involved in the particular negligent act could be dismissed individually from a lawsuit involving a partner of the partnership. Such a physician would not be liable in his individual capacity for the tort of his partner, although he would be liable in his capacity as a partner of the professional association. See *Keech v. Mead Johnson and Co.* (Pa.Super.1990).

Partners may also be held liable for the negligence of their employees or agents. For example, in *Brown v. Moore* (3d Cir.1957), the federal district court held that partners who maintained a sanitarium could be liable for the negligence of its medical director which resulted in the death of a patient, because the sanitarium held out that the director was an agent of the owners of the sanitarium. Respondeat superior would apply and the negligence of the employee or agent would be imputed to the partners because of this "holding out" of employment. However, *Brown* relied upon a "holding out" or "apparent agency" theory of liability that is distinct from respondeat superior. *See also Drexel v. Union Prescription Centers, Inc.* (3d Cir.1978).

B. THE PROFESSIONAL CORPORATION

The corporation (including the professional corporation) or professional limited liability company ("PLLC") are alternate forms of professional association which can be selected for organizational purposes. The liability of the shareholders or, in the case of the PLLC, the members, and the legal entity itself, is governed by the laws of the state where the corporation or PLLC is organized. All states have specific statutes which govern the formation of corporations and PLLCs and include the common forms of organization for health providers. The decision of an individual physician about whether to operate as a partnership, a corporation or a PLLC, is frequently based upon the cost of doing so, as well as the particular features of the applicable law. Generally, the larger the group of practitioners, the more advantageous it will be to form a corporation or a PLLC.

The major incentive for organizing as a corporation or as an PLLC is that the liability of the shareholders or members is limited to the value of the assets of the entity. The corporation or PLLC will not shield a physician from liability for his own negligence, but usually will protect an individual physician from liability for the medical malpractice of another physician in the corporation. See Health Care in the '90s and Beyond: Practice Structure, Competition, Government Regulation, and Malpractice Concerns, C470 ALI–ABA 41 (1989). On the other hand, the corporation may be held liable for the negligence of an individual member under respondeat superior or an agency theory. See *McGuire v. Sifers* (Kan.1984), *Medi–Stat, Inc. v. Kusturin* (Ark.1990). Depending upon the jurisdiction, the corporation (or PLLC) itself may or may not need to be insured for the negligence of an individual member.

Historically, in many jurisdictions physician organizations were barred from practicing medicine under a common law doctrine known as the "Corporate Practice of Medicine" doctrine. This doctrine originated out of concern that patients would receive inferior care if corporations have any control over physicians' medical judgment. As stated by the court in *Pediatric Neurosurgery, P.C. v. Russell* (Colo.2002), this doctrine rests on the principle "that only a person, not a corporation, may practice medicine because it is impossible for a fictional entity, a corporation, to perform medical actions or to be licensed to practice medicine." States such as Massachusetts, Colorado, New York, and others have since enacted very narrow laws allowing physicians to organize as corporate entities, thus creating a statutory exception to the common law rule that corporations may not practice medicine. These laws are very specific in requiring all shareholders (or members) to be licensed physicians. The effect of these statutory exceptions is to impute liability to a corporation when one of its member physicians has been negligent. *See Pediatric Neurosurgery, P.C. v. Russell* (Colo.2002). In this case, the plaintiff sued the defendant corporation for the negligent acts of two of its doctors in treating the plaintiff, who was born with spina bifida. The Colorado Supreme Court overturned the lower court, holding that Colorado state law, creating an exception to the Corporate Practice of Medicine doctrine, contemplates that professional corporations may practice medicine, have control over medical matters, and be vicariously liable for the negligent acts of its employees.

A related liability issue is whether a corporate stockholder, director, agent or employee of the corporation would be personally liable for the torts of a physician member of the corporation. For example, patients have attempted to sue individually non-treating physicians who were members of a professional corporation for the malpractice of a physician with whom they were associated. *Birt v. St. Mary Mercy Hospital of Gary, Inc. et al.* (Ind.App.1977) involved a medical corporation of physicians which was hired to staff the emergency room of the hospital. The plaintiff alleged that he was treated negligently by one of the corporation's physicians. The court held that physicians associated with the treating physician were not individually liable for negligence merely by virtue of being officers or having holdings in the corporation. Individual liability would require malfeasance on the part of the individual physician. *Birt's* interpretation of the statute was consistent with the common law of the Indiana.

In some situations, the negligence of a physician results in suit against an organization with which he is not directly associated nor maintains employee status. For example, a managing corporation operating on behalf of a hospital may or may not be liable for the negligence of a physician who treats patients at the hospital. Such liability usually depends upon agency principles, i.e., whether the management corporation has the requisite degree of supervision and control over the physician. See *Noble v. Porter* (N.Y.A.D.1992).

As discussed, the scope of liability of a corporation or PLLC and its members will depend upon common law and statutory provisions, as well as the particular facts of the case. In addition, principles of agency may be applied in those cases where a negligent physician is not a member of the corporation or the PLLC. In any event, unlike a partnership (discussed above), both the corporate form of organization and the PLLC minimize individual liability on behalf of a member who does not in any way participate in another member's negligent act.

CHAPTER EIGHT

HOSPITAL LIABILITY

I. IN GENERAL THE ROOTS OF HOSPITAL LIABILITY

A. RESPONDEAT SUPERIOR

Historically hospitals, as charitable institutions, were afforded absolute immunity from tort liability. In *Schloendorff v. Society of N.Y. Hospital* (N.Y. 1914) the court held that hospital liability for the negligence of its employees depends on whether the causative act of the injury was "administrative" or "medical". Administrative acts were considered to be those in the realm of hospital control, whereas medical acts were not. This naturally gave rise to many inconsistencies in interpretation of what exactly constituted medical or administrative tasks. Notwithstanding the difficulties in interpretation, the basic underlying issue was whether or not the hospital could be deemed to have any control over the particular act involved.

As the nature and public perception of the hospital institution has changed, liability of the hospital for the negligent acts of its staff has emerged as a viable claim. As the court in *Schloendorff* explained, "hospitals have evolved into highly sophisticated corporations operating primarily on a fee-for-service basis. The corporate hospital of today has assumed the role of a comprehensive health center with responsibility for arranging and coordinating the total health care of its patients."

As established by the New York Court in *Bing v. Thunig* (N.Y.1957), hospitals are no longer exempt from rules of liability based on respondeat superior. In *Bing*, a woman was burned during an operation as a result of a surgeon's use of electro-cautery. The bed linen ignited during the operation as it had been contaminated by a zephiren solution during the nurses' preparation of the patient for surgery. The patient sued both the surgeon and the hospital. The court allowed recovery against both, holding that the hospital should bear the same burden as other employers, including responsibility for negligent acts of its employees committed within the scope of their employment. *Bing v. Thunig* (N.Y. 1957).

In *Bing*, the court provided a succinct summary of what was then the state of the law as well as its rationale for abandoning the traditional rule. Aside from charitable considerations, the court also rejected hospital liability based on traditional principles of respondeat superior since the staff (physicians, nurses and other skilled professionals) was considered akin to independent contractors. As such, they perform patient care functions with that level of skill required for their profession. Consequently, the hospital, being unable to control these professionals or dictate the course of the treatment provided, could not be held liable for its employees' negligence.

Today, the public expectation of the hospital reaches far beyond providing a facility for medical treatment; it is a full service institution with responsibility for all aspects of patient care. Because of this heightened expectation, courts are more willing to hold hospitals liable for the negligence of their employees, including physicians. In *Johnson v. LeBonheur Children's Medical Center* (Tenn.2002), the Tennessee Supreme Court held a private hospital vicariously liable under the doctrine of respondeat superior for the negligence of two resident physicians performing surgery on a young patient. In *Johnson*, the patient sustained permanent neurological damage due to cardiac arrest during surgery. In finding the hospital liable under respondeat superior, the court held that a statute immunizing state employees from liability for negligence would not protect a private hospital even though the residents employed at the hospital were paid employees of the state. The court applied a theory of dual agency and held the private hospital to be a master separate from the state.

While a defendant must be an actual employee of the hospital for the hospital to be liable under respondeat superior, hospitals have been held liable as licensees for negligence in allowing a non-employee, non-physician access to the hospital for the purpose of examining patients. In *Heffern v. University of Cincinnati Hospital* (Ohio App.2001), a man known as "Dr. West" was examining and treating patients at University of Cincinnati Hospital despite the fact the he was not a physician. This was discovered when he falsely diagnosed a patient as having Chlamydia and being pregnant despite the fact that neither diagnosis was correct. While not liable for the criminal acts of this imposter, the Court of Appeals in Ohio held the hospital liable as licensee for negligently granting the phony doctor access to the hospital's emergency department and examination rooms and giving him the opportunity to examine patients.

B.   EMPLOYEES AND INDEPENDENT CONTRACTORS

Early decisions concerning hospital liability did not address its potential liability for negligence of the professional staff who generally receive no economic compensation from the hospital. These professionals may include the staff physicians who are not paid by the hospital but instead exchange their services for "staff privileges", i.e., the ability to admit patients to the hospital and provide care for them within the hospital. Staff physicians may also include physicians or other professionals who perform certain specialties such as emergency medicine, anesthesia, radiology, or pathology through a contract with the hospital to provide such services. Typically patients are billed directly.

Another variation on the theme occurs when specialty services are performed for the hospital and are compensated on a contract rather than salary basis. For purposes of liability, services performed within these types of arrangements are generally considered to be those of an independent contractor. The critical factor in determining whether such professionals are "employees" or "independent contractors" is the institution's "right to control" their conduct and activity. Restatement (Agency) 2d sec. 2. Since the hospital does not generally retain a right to control the manner in which they practice their profession, but only to terminate the contract usually they are deemed to be independent contractors.

In determining whether there is a "right of control" in order to classify a provider of care as an employee or independent contractor, some jurisdictions will consider other factors besides the economic relationship. For example, some will inquire about whether an agency relationship was intended, whether there is independent ownership, whether the service involves a distinct occupation, and whether special skill is needed to perform the work. See *Menzie v. Windham Community Memorial Hospital* (D.Conn.1991). The Restatement (Agency) 2d also considers such factors as whether the worker supplies the tools and instrumentalities needed, the length of time of the employment, and whether the particular occupation is typically done by a specialist without supervision. (Restatement (Agency) 2d sec. 220.)

A few jurisdictions have been reluctant to impute the liability of a physician to the hospital under any circumstance on the basis that hospitals are "powerless" to command or forbid any acts within the professional practice of the physician. See *Banks v. St. Mary's Hospital and Medical Center* (D.Colo. 1983). This, of course, does not preclude the possibility of a negligence action against the hospital based upon its own tortious acts.

II. VICARIOUS LIABILITY

A. OSTENSIBLE OR APPARENT AGENCY

The doctrine of ostensible agency or apparent authority has been the predominant theory upon which to base an action for vicarious liability against a hospital for the negligence of independent contractors. As stated in the Restatement (Second) of Torts § 429, "One who employs an independent contractor to perform services for another which are accepted in the reasonable belief that the services are being rendered by the employer or by his servants, is subject to liability for physical harm caused by the negligence of the contract or in supplying such services, to the same extent as though the employer were supplying them himself or by his servants." This section of the Restatement suggests an exception to the general rule that a hospital incurs no liability for the negligence of independent contractors but only for those who provide care within the traditional employment relationship. In *Simmons v. Tuomey Regional Medical Center* (S.C. 2000), the court adopted this section of the Restatement, holding that a hospital has a nondelegable duty with regard to the physicians who practice in their emergency rooms. In order to prove this duty, the plaintiff must show that (1) the hospital held itself out to the public by offering to provide services; (2) the plaintiff looked to the hospital, rather than the individual physician, for care; and (3) a person in similar circumstances reasonably would have believed that the physician who treated him or her was a hospital employee. Courts intentionally limit recovery under this theory to situations in which a patient seeks services at the hospital as an institution, and is treated by a physician who reasonably appears to be a hospital employee.

Yet another potential basis of liability can be derived from the Restatement (Agency) 2d which recognizes "agency by estoppel". To meet this standard, there must be evidence of justifiable reliance by the patient on the representations of the hospital that care is provided by servants or agents of the hospital. This additional element of reliance makes agency by estoppel a stricter standard than that required by the tort theory of ostensible agency. See *Walker v. Winchester Memorial Hospital* (W.D.Va. 1984).

B. NON–DELEGABLE DUTIES

The cases which consistently support use of the doctrine of ostensible agency are those involving care provided by physicians through the hospital emergency room. One such case involved the alleged wrongful death of a woman treated in a hospital emergency room which was staffed by a group of physicians who delivered emergency services through a contract with the hospital. See *Stewart v. Midani* (N.D.Ga.1981). Several factors were identified to justify a patient assuming that there existed an agency relationship between the hospital and the emergency room group. Specifically, the patient signed a hospital release form; the patient was referred to as a patient of the hospital on the indemnification agreement; the patient was billed by the hospital, with payment to be submitted to the hospital; the appearance of the emergency room was that it was an integral part of the hospital. *Stewart*. These actions were held to indicate that the hospital was representing the physician as its agent.

Other factors will also affect the existence of an agency relationship. A person entering through the emergency room is unaware of the relationships between the health care professionals who care for them, particularly when entering with an emergency or crisis situation. Usually patients cannot be expected to inquire about the facility's organizational structure or to make decisions based upon such inquiry. The *Stewart* court concluded that unless the hospital notifies patients as to the status of its caregivers, or unless patients are treated by their own personal physicians who meet them at the facility, the patient may justifiably rely on the apparent authority of the physicians as agents of the hospital. Therefore, the hospital could be held responsible for any injury resulting from that care. *Stewart*.

In *Walker v. Winchester Memorial Hospital* (W.D.Va.1984), the federal district court found the reasoning of *Stewart* persuasive, finding not only that the hospital "held out" or represented that the physicians were agents of the hospital, but also that the patient relied on that representation to its detriment. The fact that the patient was comatose upon arriving at the emergency room and continued in that condition for several days weighed against a finding of reliance; however, the court left the issue for the jury. The requirement of reliance under agency principles is seemingly more difficult to prove.

A divergence from this stricter standard is illustrated by *Martell v. St. Charles Hospital* (N.Y.Sup. 1987), where the hospital was held to be vicariously liable for the treatment given by physicians in the emergency room. As the court explained, "patients in this situation have looked to the hospital as the provider of medical services, the hospital has given the appearance that it is the provider of the medical services and the patient has reasonably relied on that appearance." The court held, for policy reasons, that agency principles should not be strictly adhered to as they would provide hospitals with a shield against liability. *Martell* held that "the law of New York should be that hospitals are liable for the malpractice of physicians in hospital emergency rooms irrespective of private contractual relationships between the physicians and the hospitals and without regard for whether the patient has reason not to rely upon the appearance that the physician is a hospital employee."

In the same year, *Jackson v. Power* (Alaska 1987), affirmed reliance on basic principles of agency law and also found a basis for potential liability of hospitals for emergency room physicians through traditional exceptions to the non-liability of independent contractors. *Jackson* involved a boy who was injured due to a fall from a cliff. He suffered multiple injuries including internal damage. The emergency room doctor ordered no tests to determine the status of his kidneys and the boy ultimately lost both kidneys. The court pointed out that it was the conduct of the principal (hospital) which caused a third person (patient) to trust that the agent (physician) had the authority to act for the principal. Accordingly, liability was found. The court held that the patient need not prove that the hospital specifically represented that the physician was an employee or that the patient relied upon such representation, unless there was evidence that the patient "knew or should have known" that the treating physician was not an employee.

An established exception to the rule of "no liability" for the negligence of an independent contractor is the finding of a non-delegable duty. This issue arose in *Jackson:* whether the hospital had a non-delegable duty to provide emergency room services. Based on state regulations, the Joint Committee on Accreditation of Healthcare Organizations (JCAHO) standards and hospital bylaws, *Jackson* held that a general acute care hospital has a non-delegable duty to provide emergency care. State regulations require that a physician be available to provide emergency care on a 24–hour basis. JCAHO mandates that an emergency plan be in place, and that the hospital direct and review the quality of care, as well as provide written policies and procedures for emergency services. In Jackson, the hospital bylaws also provided for the regulation and supervision of the emergency department. The result was that the duty was found to be non-delegable, and the hospital was liable for the adverse consequences of any negligent care provided.

The principle that a hospital incurs duties that are non-delegable has been applied to other medical specialties such as anesthesia and radiology. Application of the theory of ostensible agency has been variable. For instance, in *Gamble v. United States* (N.D.Ohio 1986), a patient died following what was believed to have been a cardiorespiratory arrest incident to endotracheal intubation during surgery at a Veteran's Administration hospital. The anesthesia services were provided independently through a contract with the Veteran's Administration. As the hospital held itself out as a full-service institution, including a provider of anesthesia, the court held that it could be liable for negligent provision of services. The hospital was held to have induced patients to rely on the full care provided by the hospital. Additionally, the anesthesiologist involved was the Chief of Anesthesia who also maintained an office within the hospital.

On the other hand, in *Menzie v. Windham Community Memorial Hospital* (D.Conn.1991), the court found no liability on the part of the hospital for negligent anesthesia services provided by so-called independent contractors. These independent contractors received no compensation or benefits from the hospital and carried their own malpractice insurance. The court found that the hospital did not exert any control over their practice, since only an executive committee of staff doctors evaluated the quality of their care. The hospital did not do so directly. The court held that the hospital could not be held liable on an apparent agency theory as the requisite element of reliance was absent. Additionally, the court appeared to require direct evidence of reliance such as the hospital leading patients to believe that the physicians were employees. *Menzie* further held that the hospital did not have a non-delegable duty to provide anesthesia or other services. The court found only that "[t]he hospital's duty is to provide a place for treatment and ensure the availability of treatment."

The varying rules applicable to anesthesiology appear to also apply to radiology. Thus liability for radiology services will not typically be imposed on the hospital if provided by independent contractors. For instance, in *Royer v. St. Paul Fire & Marine Insurance Co.* (La.App.1987), the court held there was no vicarious liability of the hospital on behalf of a radiologist who was allegedly negligent while performing an arteriogram. The hospital had a contract with an independent radiology clinic which provided equipment, employed its own technicians and handled its own billing, insurance, and workmen's compensation. Principles of non-delegable duty were also rejected.

In another case involving a radiologist in a rural area who travelled from hospital to hospital, a Montana court refused to find an agency relationship despite the hospital having provided the radiologist with an office, equipment and personnel, and handling all of the billing. The court declined to find liability under a theory of vicarious liability for a non-delegable duty. See *Estate of Milliron v. Francke* (Mont.1990). This, of course, does not necessarily mean that a radiologist employed by a hospital who performs negligently might not subject the hospital to liability under principles of vicarious liability. See *Daly v. United States* (9th Cir.1991).

C. SCOPE OF LIABILITY

Under some circumstances, a hospital may be held vicariously liable for the negligence of a physician outside of the scope of the traditional physician-patient relationship. For example, a duty to warn the patient of an abnormality detected during an employment physical exam was imposed in *Daly v. United States* (9th Cir.1991). In *Daly*, a Veteran's Administration hospital radiologist neglected to inform a patient of the results of an x-ray taken during a routine physical examination. The patient later suffered permanent lung damage which could have been avoided had the condition been diagnosed in a timely manner. The court held that the Veteran's Administration hospital could also be held liable for injury resulting from negligence. To the extent that physicians may be liable under such circumstances, liability may also extend to a hospital with whom the physician has the requisite relationship.

D. THE PETRILLO DOCTRINE

In defending a hospital against a claim of vicarious liability for injury resulting from its physicians' negligent care, there are certain procedural considerations that may become significant. The landmark case of *Petrillo v. Syntex Laboratories* (Ill. App.1986), involved a product liability action against Syntex Laboratories, the manufacturer of two infant formulas, for injuries which arose following the plaintiff's consumption of the formula. The hospital's attorney discussed the matter with the patient's treating physician. Criticizing that discussion, the *Petrillo* court held that "the defense attorney's *ex parte* discussions with patient's treating physicians which were done without the patient's consent and which were not performed pursuant to authorized methods of discovery, violated public policy favoring physician-patient confidentiality as reflected in the code of ethics of medical profession and favoring fiduciary nature of relationship between patient and treating physician."

Petrillo, however, has subsequently been limited in its application by *Morgan v. Count of Cook* (Ill.

App.1993). In *Morgan*, where the hospital and physician were both defendants, the court held that the hospital is included within the physician-patient privilege, as the patient is deemed to have impliedly consented to the release of his medical information to the hospital. Thus in *Morgan, ex parte* discussions between the patient's treating physician and counsel for the hospital were permissible.

The distinction, of course, was that *Morgan* involved a situation where the hospital was defending itself against actions of its own physician who treated the patient, as opposed to *Petrillo* which dealt with the hospital defending itself for the actions of its employee. The *Petrillo* rule places the hospital in a difficult situation: the hospital must go through the formalities of discovery and may not even be able to acquire the information needed to defend itself. The defense attorneys are barred from communicating directly with the physician (whose own actions may have contributed to the injury). To avoid this disadvantage to the defense, *Morgan* held that since the hospital is vicariously liable for the conduct of a physician, the physician-patient privilege is impliedly waived. Therefore, attorneys defending the hospital for such acts of negligence would have free access to communicate with the physician.

Petrillo has been further limited in situations where the hospital is a party to the lawsuit, but the hospital's medical staff, agents, and employees who provided health care to the plaintiff are not named as defendants in the plaintiff's complaint. *Burger v.*

Lutheran General Hospital et. al. (Ill.2001). In this case, the plaintiff alleged that the hospital itself was negligent in several respects in the care it provided in the emergency room and in a resulting admission to the hospital. The plaintiff then sought an emergency motion to bar communication between the Hospital's counsel and those members of its staff, agents, and employees who, although provided care, were not defendants in the suit. The court held that the hospital is not a third party with respect to its own medical information compiled by its own caregivers, and held that limited intra-hospital communication of information that is already part of the hospital and known to the hospital's agents, including hospital counsel, irrespective of the filing of a lawsuit, is permitted. "If a patient files a lawsuit against a hospital, the patient cannot validly claim any greater expectation of privacy after the lawsuit is filed than prior to its filing."

III. CORPORATE RESPONSIBILITY

A. GENERAL DUTY OF CARE, CUSTODY AND SUPERVISION

Generally, the theory of corporate liability of a hospital is based upon a duty of care, custody and supervision by the hospital and its staff to its patients. Although this duty will typically be carried out by one or more individual staff members, the hospital may be directly responsible to the patient for ensuring the staff is adequately selected, trained and monitored.

As one court pointed out, the hospital does not insure the safety of the patient who is admitted to the hospital, but it does insure that patient care is conducted in accordance with reasonable standards consistent with the condition of the patient. See *Mounds Park Hospital v. Von Eye* (8th Cir.1957). These duties may include the exercise of ordinary care in the custody and supervision of the patient. For example, the court in *Mounds Park* held the hospital negligent when a patient jumped from a second floor window after orders were left by the physicians to observe the patient closely.

In *Wooten v. United States* (W.D.Tenn.1982), the court held the hospital's duty of reasonable care was breached when a patient was permitted to leave his bed and subsequently fell. The hospital's liability resulted from failure to raise the side rails on the patient's bed in view of the age, condition, and medication requirements of the patient. Thus, today the hospital does more than furnish a facility for care and treatment; it is directly involved in the care and management of patients.

This duty may also encompass other health and safety concerns such as providing wholesome food, protecting patients from assault and the spread of communicable disease, and ensuring that patients are in a safe building with adequate ventilation and emergency exits.

B.　DUTY TO PROVIDE EQUIPMENT AND SUPPLIES

Often reasonable and adequate care of the patient depends upon the availability of adequate equipment and supplies. In *Emory University v. Porter* (Ga.App.1961), the court clearly articulated the majority rule concerning equipment and supplies. In *Porter*, an infant, lying in a heated incubator, was burned on the foot by a light bulb inside the incubator. The incubator was an older model which allegedly did not provide precise heat control or shielding from the heat mechanism. Although the unit was under the control of the attending physician, the plaintiff did not allege negligence on his behalf. The court held that the hospital was not required to furnish the latest or most up-to-date equipment, or to incorporate all possible improvements in existing equipment. According to that court, the appliance, which was not state of the art, was not necessarily defective.

C.　LIABILITY FOR CORPORATE NEGLIGENCE

The theory of corporate negligence, as originally introduced in 1964, has expanded hospital liability for the medical care and patient services provided by physicians or others, including employees and independent contractors. Pursuant to the theory the hospital is charged with certain responsibilities that are owed directly to the patient regarding services provided within the facility.

The leading case establishing the theory of corporate negligence is *Darling v. Charleston Community Memorial Hospital* (Ill.1965). *Darling* involved a boy with multiple leg fractures who was treated by an on-call emergency room physician. The physician applied a plaster cast and admitted the patient to the hospital, but the physician never consulted an orthopedist to review his treatment. Within days, the nurses observed that the patient's toes became dark in color, swollen and a strong odor was emitted from the cast. Although adjustments were made in the cast by the same physician, the condition of the leg worsened. When the patient was finally transferred to another hospital, the leg had become gangrenous and ultimately had to be amputated eight inches below the knee.

In the suit that followed, the plaintiff brought an action directly against the hospital where he was originally treated. The patient alleged that the professional competency of the medical and nursing staff was the responsibility of the hospital. In particular, the plaintiff alleged that the emergency room physician was not trained to treat a complicated fracture, and he should have consulted a specialist. The plaintiff's position was that the duty of care of a licensed and accredited facility was established by licensing regulations, accreditation standards, and its own bylaws. As noted by the court, these administrative guidelines help define the standard of conduct necessary to fulfill that duty. Neither custom nor regulations were held to be conclusive in establishing a duty, but the rules and regulations may help the jury decide what was feasible and what the hospital knew or should have known concerning its responsibilities for the patient.

In *Darling*, the allegations, which were supported by the regulations, standards and bylaws of the hospital, were that the hospital failed to have sufficient nurses trained to recognize the gangrenous condition of the leg. Further, the hospital failed to require consultation or review of the treatment rendered by the on-call emergency room physician. According to the court, either of these grounds would support the jury verdict that the hospital was negligent.

Subsequent cases have classified the duties of the hospital into four general areas. These are: (1) a duty to use reasonable care in the maintenance of safe and adequate facilities and equipment; (2) a duty to select and retain only competent physicians; (3) a duty to oversee all persons who practice medicine or engage in patient care; and (4) a duty to formulate, adopt and enforce adequate rules and policies to ensure quality care for all patients. See *Thompson v. Nason Hospital* (Pa.1991). The principles of corporate negligence enunciated in *Thompson* have been extended by the court to apply also to nursing homes. *See Aptekman v. Philadelphia* (E.D.Pa.2001). However, courts generally have refused to extend *Thompson* and the corporate negligence doctrine to specialty physicians' practices. *See Dowhouer v. Judson* (Pa.Com.Pl.2000).

The duty to select and retain only competent physicians was illustrated in *Purcell v. Zimbelman* (Ariz.App.1972). In *Purcell*, the plaintiff brought a malpractice action against a physician treating his condition, and against the hospital for granting staff privileges to a physician whom it should have known was not competent. According to *Purcell*, the hospital owes certain duties directly to a patient, which are defined as non-delegable by licensing regulations, accreditation standards and hospital bylaws. In an accredited facility, the governing body (i.e., board of trustees) has ultimate responsibility for the quality of patient care. If, as in *Purcell*, the hospital assigns review and/or supervision of the physicians to a particular department, such assignment does not release the hospital from direct responsibility and liability for negligence. The court held that "the department of surgery was acting for and on behalf of the hospital in fulfilling this duty and if the department was negligent in not taking any action against Purcell or recommending to the board of trustees that action would be taken, then the hospital would also be negligent."

In order for the hospital to become liable under a theory of corporate negligence, there must be evidence that it had actual or constructive notice of the defect or process which created the harm. Actual or constructive notice may be obtained through information regarding staff physicians' patient care, peer review procedures, previous complaints, lawsuits or other evidence of substandard care. Additionally, the negligence attributed to the hospital must be found to have been a substantial factor in bringing about the harm to the patient. See *Thompson*.

In *Purcell*, the surgeon performed a particular procedure on a patient without waiting for the results of a biopsy or frozen section. The patient actually had a less serious condition which warranted a less drastic procedure. As a result, the patient suffered the loss of a kidney, a permanent colostomy, and urinary problems. The court admitted testimony regarding two prior malpractice suits against the surgeon. They were held to be evidence of notice to the hospital that the doctor was unskilled in this area. According to the court, it was customary for hospitals to review, through committees, the practice of staff physicians and to restrict or suspend those who do not demonstrate competency in a particular area. Again, this duty is non-delegable and ultimately remains the responsibility of the hospital. See *Purcell*.

The operation of the notice requirement is illustrated in *Thompson v. Nason Hospital* (Pa.1991). In *Thompson*, a woman was transported to the hospital emergency room following a car accident. Due to multiple trauma and a history of heart disease, she was admitted to the intensive care unit. The next day the patient was unable to move her left foot due to an intracerebral hematoma. The surgeon, however, attributed this to a neurological problem and did not investigate further despite the fact the patient was on anticoagulants and exhibiting bleeding in her eye. See *Thompson*.

The court stated that if a physician fails to act after abnormalities are reported, custom and hospital policy should require that the situation be reported to the authorities of the hospital so that corrective action can be taken. *Thompson*. Such a requirement would put the hospital on constructive notice that the physician was not handling the patient appropriately. If, for example, there had been a failure to report a variation from standard practice and the patient was injured as a result, liability of the hospital may result.

To establish liability on the part of a hospital, causation must also be proven. According to *Purcell*, the plaintiff "must introduce evidence that it was more likely than not that the conduct of the defendant was a substantial factor in bringing about the result." Thus, the plaintiff must prove that the negligence of the hospital was "substantial" in causing the injury. As *Purcell*, stated, "[w]e believe it reasonably probable to conclude that had the hospital taken some action against Dr. Purcell, whether in the form of suspension, remonstration, restriction or other means, the surgical procedure utilized in this case would not have been undertaken by the doctor and Mr. Zimbelman would not have been injured."

The requirements of notice and causation potentially limit the liability of the hospital even where negligence on the part of the physician or the hospital is found. For example, in *Bost v. Riley* (N.C.App. 1980), where a physician failed to keep adequate progress notes, the court found that the hospital

violated its duty in not taking appropriate corrective action. However, as no evidence was offered
that this omission contributed to the death of the
patient, the hospital could not be held liable. See
also *Walls v. Hazleton State General Hospital* (Pa.
Cmwlth.1993), which held that the negligence of a
physician does not automatically give rise to liability of the hospital for corporate negligence. In *Walls*,
the court held that expert testimony is required to
establish that the conduct of hospital caused harm
to the patient. Although it appeared that a physician failed to keep a Wagner fixation device tight-
ened which resulted in a separation of the patient's
fracture, the court held that evidence would also be
required to establish that the failure of the radiologist to notify the surgeon of the separation was a
substantial factor in causing harm. As no causal
connection between the hospital and harm was
demonstrated, the hospital could not be held liable
on a theory of corporate negligence.

Other factors, depending upon state law, also
affect application of the theory of corporate negligence. For instance, Kansas has rejected a theory of
corporate negligence that imposes liability on a hospital for failing to select and retain only competent
physicians. See *McVay v. Rich* (Kan.App.1993). The
Kansas statute, K.S.A. 1992 Supp. 40–3403 (which
established The Health Care Stabilization Fund),
has been interpreted to limit the liability of health
care providers and medical facilities who are covered or insured under the fund. It provides that in
cases involving an independent contractor, who is

qualified under the fund, the hospital "shall have no vicarious liability or responsibility for any injury arising out of the rendering of or failure to render professional services by another health care provider who is also covered by the fund." According to *McVay*, this applies even if a hospital were negligent in the screening of physicians and should have known that a physician was not competent. The apparent policy reason for this statutory provision is the attempt to stabilize liability insurance rates by preventing multiple parties from being liable for any one occurrence.

IV. EMERGENCY TREATMENT AND ACTIVE LABOR ACT (EMTALA)

The Emergency Medical Treatment and Active Labor Act ("EMTALA") is a provision originally established under the Consolidated Omnibus Budget Reconciliation Act of 1986 ("COBRA") requiring hospitals to provide emergency care and to provide emergency department services as a prerequisite to receiving Medicare funding. 42 U.S.C. § 1395dd. EMTALA was created to ensure equal availability of emergency care to all patients regardless of their ability to pay. EMTALA is not intended to create a federal medical malpractice statute, and courts have refused to impute liability under EMTALA to individual physicians for their medical negligences. See *Correa Ortiz v. Sile* (D.P.R.2002). As a result of EMTALA, hospitals emergency departments are responsible for adequately screening all patients, and for treating and stabilizing them prior to any transfer from the facility. The statute, which applies to all patients, is intended to deter 'patient dumping,'—the practice of refusing care to patients who lack the ability to pay.

The EMTALA statute proscribes three specific areas of hospital responsibility: (1) to provide appropriate screening for emergency conditions for people who come to the emergency department; (2) to provide appropriate stabilization of anyone determined to have an emergency medical condition, and (3) to provide for an appropriate transfer in situations where it is determined a patient must be transferred to another facility.

A. SCREENING REQUIREMENT

The first subsection of EMTALA requires hospital emergency departments to "provide for an appropriate medical screening examination within the capability of the hospital's emergency department, including ancillary services routinely available to the emergency department, to determine whether or not an emergency medical condition exists." *See* 42 U.S.C. § 1395dd(a). While the statute calls for an "appropriate medical screening", a negligent misdiagnosis will not subject the hospital to liability under EMTALA. See *Battle v. Memorial Hospital at Gulfport* (5th Cir.2000). In *Battle*, a baby was permanently brain damaged after a physician in a hospital emergency room misdiagnosed the baby's encephalitic condition as febrile seizures. In dismissing the EMTALA claims against the hospital, the Fifth Circuit stated that in order for a plaintiff to prevail based upon a failure to screen theory, it must show that the hospital treated the patient differently from other patients with similar symptoms. If the plaintiff cannot meet this burden, he fails to establish that he received disparate treatment in violation of EMTALA's screening requirement.

Hospitals will not be held liable under EMTALA for going above and beyond the duties proscribed by the statute. As the Ninth Circuit held in *Baker v. Adventist Health, Inc.* (9th Cir.2001), a hospital is not liable under EMTALA for calling in an outside expert to provide a screening examination that was beyond the hospital's capabilities. In *Baker*, the plaintiff was brought to a hospital's emergency room for a mental health evaluation and the hospital called on an outside physician to perform this evaluation because the hospital staff lacked a qualified mental health care provider. The outside examining physician determined that the patient did not constitute a danger to himself or others and discharged the patient. The patient was found dead hanging in a tree two days later. When the decedent's family brought a suit against the hospital for failure to screen with one of its own physicians, the court refused to hold the hospital liable under EMTALA, noting that the hospital did not have a duty to provide a mental health screening. Mental health services were not listed in the hospital's written policy detailing ancillary services available at the emergency department and calling in an outside physician to perform the examination was held to be beyond the liability of the hospital.

B. STABILIZATION REQUIREMENT

Under 42 U.S.C. § 1395dd(b) if any individual comes to a hospital and the hospital determines that the individual has an emergency medical condition, the hospital must try to stabilize that condition. However, the circuit courts are split regarding to when this stabilization requirement is applicable and when the requirement ends.

The Sixth Circuit has suggested that EMTALA's stabilization requirement is not limited to the time of presentment to the emergency department, and an EMTALA violation might occur even after the patient is admitted and hospitalized for a number of days. *See Thornton v. Southwest Detroit Hosp.* (6th Cir.1990). In *Thornton*, a patient who had suffered a stroke had been in the hospital for 21 days and it was determined that the patient needed further long term care. However, the hospital discharged the patient when a rehabilitation facility refused to admit the patient for post-stroke rehabilitation because his health insurer would not cover the cost of treatment. The patient was discharged from the hospital and her condition seriously deteriorated.

The Sixth Circuit did not hold the defendant hospital liable in *Thornton* because it determined that in this instance, the patient had been stabilized. However, the court went on to state that the stabilization requirement does not end at admission, and a hospital may not circumvent the stabilization requirement by admitting the patient and immediately discharging that patient. The First Circuit has joined the Fourth Circuit in holding that the stabilization requirement of EMTALA extends beyond the emergency department and into the main hospital. *See Lopez–Soto v. Hawayek* (1st Cir. 1999).

Other circuits have refused to extend the stabilization requirement beyond the emergency department, holding that the requirement ends on admission or applies only when a patient is transferred. In *Bryant v. Adventist Health Sys./West Redbud Community Hosp. Dist.* (9th Cir.2002), the emergency room physician failed to detect a lung abscess and released a patient after injecting him with medication and prescribing antibiotics. The patient was admitted to that same hospital the next day, then transferred to a second hospital for an operation. He died shortly after being discharged from the second hospital, and the decedent's estate brought a suit alleging violation of EMTALA by the first hospital for failing to stabilize the patient while he was admitted at that hospital.

The Ninth Circuit refused to extend EMTALA's stabilization requirement to admission, holding that "EMTALA's stabilization requirement ends when an individual is admitted for impatient care." Under these circumstances, instances of negligent post admission care should be redressed through state tort law, as EMTALA is not intended to establish a federal standard of care or a federal malpractice cause of action. The court refused to accept the plaintiff's argument that such a stance will cause hospitals to use the hospital admission process as a means of circumventing EMTALA. The Eleventh Circuit has taken a similar approach in addressing EMTALA's stabilization requirement. *See Harry v. Marchant* (11th Cir.2002).

C. TRANSFER REQUIREMENT

In addition to the stabilization requirement, EM-TALA requires the hospital to meet certain conditions in order to properly effectuate the transfer of a patient from its emergency department to another facility. The individual or person responsible for the person being transferred must request the transfer in writing, or a physician must determine that the risks of transfer are outweighed by the medical benefits reasonably expected to be provided at another medical facility, and this determination must be documented in a signed certification. *See* 42 U.S.C. § 1395dd(c)(1). Finally, the transfer must be "appropriate," which is statutorily defined as a transfer in which the transferring hospital provides the medical treatment within its capacity which minimizes risks to the individual's health. *See* 42 U.S.C. § 1395dd(c)(2).

The certification requirement in the transfer provision is not applicable unless the hospital has actually detected an emergency condition and elects to transfer the patient rather than stabilize the condi-

tion. *See Jackson v. East Bay Hospital* (9th Cir.
2001). In *Jackson*, a patient with a psychiatric
disorder came to the emergency room with chest
pain, a sore throat, and dry heaves. The diagnosis
specifically ruled out any prescription drug toxicity
and the patient was sent home. The next day, the
patient was taken to the same emergency department after being found wandering in the road during the middle of the night. The emergency department diagnosed a psychiatric disorder and ordered
the patient transferred to a psychiatric facility.
Shortly after arrival, the patient died due to prescription drug toxicity. The patient's family brought
claims against the transferring hospital for violation
of EMTALA's certification requirement because the
certification form did not contain specific reference
to the risks and benefits. The Ninth Circuit affirmed the lower court, concluding that EMTALA's
certification requirement does not apply when the
hospital has failed to detect an emergency medical
condition.

In determining whether a transfer is appropriate,
the standard for minimizing the risks of transfer is
measured by a hospital's standard practices and
procedures, and a plaintiff is required to produce
evidence that existing hospital procedure was not
followed in order to prove an inappropriate transfer
under § 1395dd(c)(2). *See Ingram v. Muskogee Regional Medical Center* (10th Cir.2000). In *Ingram,*
the plaintiff suffered a gunshot wound to the chest.
Because the hospital lacked the necessary surgeons,
they elected to transfer the patient to another hos-

pital. The patient died shortly upon arrival at the transferee hospital. The patient's estate brought suit alleging the transfer was inappropriate because the defendants inappropriately transferred the patient by failing to first stabilize her condition and minimize the risk of transfer by inserting chest tubes. The Tenth Circuit affirmed the lower courts grant of summary judgment to the defendants on the EMTALA claim. The court held that a hospital determines its own capabilities by establishing a standard procedure, and an "appropriate medical screening" is achieved so long as the hospital follows this procedure. The court states that "this narrow interpretation ties the statute to its limited purpose, which was to eliminate patient dumping and not to federalize medical malpractice."

Another determination that can give rise to transferor liability is whether a patient in transit via ambulance to a hospital who is then diverted to another facility has "come to" the transferor hospital within the scope of EMTALA. *See Arrington v. Wong* (9th Cir.2001). In *Arrington*, the patient suffered a heart attack on his way to work and was in transit via ambulance to the nearest hospital when a physician at the hospital instructed the ambulance staff to transport the patient to a hospital further away. The patient died within an hour of arrival at the hospital, and the plaintiff's family sued the first hospital under EMTALA's transfer provision for failing to stabilize the patient before transferring him to another hospital.

The Ninth Circuit held that the patient had "come to" the emergency department for purposes of EMTALA when he was on his way to the hospital in the ambulance. A hospital may be held in violation of the transfer provision of EMTALA if it diverts an ambulance that has contacted its emergency room and is on its way to that hospital if the hospital is not on already diversionary status. It is not necessary that the patient actually "arrive at a hospital" to come within the auspices of EMTALA's transfer provision.

D.   IMMUNITY UNDER EMTALA

Under very limited circumstances, certain categories of hospitals have been immune from suit under EMTALA. The two most recognizable categories of hospitals are those run by the state and government hospitals on Native American reservations.

The EMTALA statute contains no clear expression of intent to abrogate Eleventh Amendment sovereign immunity, and state hospitals have been successful in defending EMTALA claims based upon Eleventh Amendment immunity. *See Drew v. University of Tennessee Regional Medical Center Hospital*, (6th Cir.2000). In *Drew*, the court held that while EMTALA preempted the relevant field of hospital regulation, it did not preempt an otherwise valid assertion of Eleventh Amendment immunity.

Similarly, hospitals operating under the Indian Health Care Improvement Act (IHCIA) are immune from suit under EMTALA for intentionally denying a non-Indian emergency medical care and failing to stabilize the person's condition. See *Williams v. United States* (4th Cir.2001). In *Williams*, the court found an express provision in the IHCIA which prohibited participating hospitals from treating non-Indians. This provision was held to constitute express immunity from suit under EMTALA for failing to provide care to a non-Indian.

CHAPTER NINE

CONTRACT, WARRANTY AND STRICT LIABILITY

I. IN GENERAL: CONTRACT-BASED CLAIMS

When an individual engages the services of a physician, a contractual relationship, express or implied, is formed. The physician represents that he possesses the qualifications of a physician and that he will use an ordinary degree of care and skill in the performance of medical services. The individual usually agrees to pay, or make other arrangements, for the services rendered by the physician. This exchange gives rise to an implied contract in law and becomes the basis for a physician-patient relationship. In order for a patient to recover from a physician on the basis of a contract theory, a patient must first establish the existence of a physician-patient relationship, express or implied. This contractual relationship between physician and patient arises even if formal contract language is not used.

During the course of the professional relationship, physicians sometimes make representations or "promises" to patients concerning anticipated results of medical treatment. For example, a plastic surgeon offering cosmetic surgery to a reluctant patient might promote the procedure by guaranteeing the patient's satisfaction and minimizing the likelihood of complications or risks. A patient who is disappointed with the result may thereafter sue for "breach of promise" to achieve the anticipated result. *See Kershak v. Pennsylvania Hospital* (E.D.Pa. 1995) and *Natale v. Meia* (Conn.Super.1998) upholding a plaintiff's right to sue for breach of contract to achieve a specific result.

Some jurisdictions, however, are reluctant to enforce this type of promise or agreement as a matter of public policy. This reluctance to enforce such agreements stems from a policy concern that if such agreements are honored, physicians will be hesitant to offer therapeutic reassurances to patients and will practice "defensive medicine." *Scarzella v. Saxon* (D.C.App.1981), quoting *Sullivan v. O'Connor* (Mass.1973). The argument in favor of recognizing this cause of action is that physicians would otherwise be free to promote unrealistic expectations without consequence. Thus, failure to assign damages might lead physicians to grossly exaggerate and misinform patients in order to secure consent.

Contract actions require clear proof as to what the physician promised. Courts have held that a plaintiff must present "clear proof" that a doctor made a promise or guarantee to the patient in order to prove the existence of an actionable contract. *Van Leeuwan v. Nuzzi* (D.Colo.1993), *Sard v. Hardy* (Md.1977).

In order to meet the burden of clear proof, courts have examined a variety of factors. Generally, courts will require that the promise be expressly made by the physician to the patient. *Scarzella.* Courts will look to the language used between the parties to determine whether any statements the physician made rise to the level of a guarantee, thus making it an actionable claim. In order to find for the plaintiff, in all contract cases for personal services the jury must determine that the physician made a specific, clear and express promise to cure or effect a specific result. *Bucalo v. University of Michigan Board of Regents,* (Mich.1989).

Some jurisdictions not only examine the language of the contract, but also require "the existence of a contract supported by separate consideration" in order to support a claim for breach of contract. *Dorney v. Harris* (D.Colo.1980), *Coleman v. Garrison* (Del.1975).

Other jurisdictions may require proof of separate consideration when the promise is made separate from or after the medical procedure. There is a distinction between a doctor's therapeutic assurances that the patient will recover which is not actionable and an express promise that a treatment will produce a specific result which is actionable. The court held that a condition precedent must be met before the defendant's performance is considered a breach of contract. *Hollmann v Putman* (Ill.App.1984). Yet, other jurisdictions require no proof of separate consideration where the promise was "an inducement to consent to the treatment."

Depenbrok v. Kaiser Foundation Health Plan (Cal. App.1978); *Hollman v Putnam.*

Finally, some jurisdictions have legislation that requires that there be a written agreement, signed by both parties, in order to support a claim for breach of contract. Mich.Comp.Laws Ann. § 566.132(g), Del. Code tit.18 § 6851 (1989) (for medical malpractice actions "no claim for breach of contract may be asserted unless such contract is in writing.")

The requirement that a plaintiff present "clear proof" of an express agreement to achieve a particular result reflects legislative intent to permit meritorious claims without requiring physicians to practice defensive medicine. A physician must have some discretion to reassure apprehensive patients without the threat of becoming insurers for the services they provide. On the other hand, physicians must be discouraged from exaggerating the benefits of a procedure in order to secure a patient's consent.

The cause of action for breach of contract is separate and distinct from the malpractice action even though they originate from the same act. The plaintiff may plead both in the alternative. Malpractice is predicated on negligence theory (failure of the physician to exercise the requisite degree of medical care and skill). It is a tort claim. The action in contract is based upon the physician's alleged failure to perform in accordance with a specific agreement. *Stewart v. Rudner* (Mich.1957).

In a malpractice action, the damages are calculated on the basis of personal injury to the plaintiff and often include the pain and suffering resulting from the tortious act. In a contract action, standard measures for recovery include "compensatory" or "expectancy" damages which are determined to be an amount that will put the patient in the same position he would have been in had the contract not been executed. These damages may include physical and mental suffering. In the alternative, the patient may elect to receive "restitution" damages which are calculated to be an amount corresponding to any benefit given to the defendant physician by the patient in regard to the contractual relationship. *Sullivan,* infra. There is no general agreement among courts as to how a patient's damages should be calculated and what should be included. Courts use their discretion in evaluating the circumstances surrounding the contract to determine what damages are compensable from the contract and whether any compensation is appropriate for psychological or physical injury.

Finally, another significant issue distinguishes tort-based claims from contract-based claims in the context of medical injuries. A contract claim usually has a statute of limitations between four and six years, while a tort action generally has a statute of limitations between one and three years, unless contrary legislation has been adopted. In those cases in which the tort statute has expired, some plaintiffs have attempted to craft their claims in contract terms to avoid the limitations issue.

II. TYPES OF CONTRACT CLAIMS

There are three types of actions that stem from a breach of contract between a doctor and patient: (1) contracts for a specific result, (2) contracts for specific procedures, and (3) contracts to perform services.

A. CONTRACT FOR SPECIFIC RESULTS

For this type of contract to arise, a physician must contract with the patient that his treatment will produce a specific end. Again, this is difficult to establish because the practice of medicine has many attendant uncertainties and human physiology is unique to each individual. *Sullivan v. O'Connor* (Mass.1973). If a contract has been made and the specific results do not follow, the patient has a potential breach of contract claim against the physician.

One way to determine whether a contract for specific results has been made is exemplified in *Guilmet v. Campbell* (Mich.1971); *Bucalo v University of Michigan Board of Regents* (Mich.1989). In *Guilmet*, the patient suffered from a peptic ulcer and consulted a physician, who recommended a vagotomy (nerve severing surgery) to remedy the problem. The doctor told the patient that this surgery would remedy the problem, that the operation was very simple, and that the patient would be out of work for no more than four weeks. The patient underwent an unsuccessful vagotomy which not only required three additional operations to correct the problem, but resulted in a series of infections as well as complications from needed blood transfusions. The patient sued the physician for malpractice and breach of contract for specific results. The jury found that the physician was not negligent but had breached the patient's contract, based solely on the testimonial evidence presented by the doctor and the patient, even though there was no writing memorializing the alleged contract and no additional consideration had been provided.

Contrast *Guilmet* with *Clevenger v. Haling* (Mass. 1979). In *Clevenger*, a patient, after having a tubal ligation in order to prevent future pregnancies, became pregnant and sued her physician for breach of contract for a specific result. In establishing whether the doctor was liable in contract , the court closely examined exactly what the physician allegedly represented to the patient in order to determine whether the parties had entered into a specific contract. Using the "clear proof" standard, recovery was denied on the basis of breach of contract for a specific result. The court determined that the doctor's statements to the patient identifying the procedure as a "permanent thing" and indicating that the plaintiff would not "have any more children after this operation" did not create a contract between the parties. The court held that the physician did not use words that were promissory in nature (i.e. "I promise you will not have any more children") and thus the patient had not sustained her burden of establishing a breach of contract.

In *Sullivan v. O'Connor* (Mass.1973), the patient, a well-known professional entertainer, agreed to surgery performed by the defendant doctor upon his promise "to perform plastic surgery on her nose and thereby enhance her beauty and improve her appearance." The surgery, disfigured the patient's nose and caused her to suffer physical and mental pain. The court determined that an express contract did exist between the doctor and the patient and that the patient was entitled to damages. Compare *Rosenblum v. Cherner* (D.C.App.1966), in which the court held that a dentist who told his patient that his dental work would "please her to her personal satisfaction" did not give rise to a contract between the physician and patient.

As mentioned above courts have imposed certain standards in order to obtain consistency and predictability among medical malpractice cases alleging contract claims. Some states have enacted specific legislation to promote uniformity of results. Such legislation usually mandates that either a writing is required or there must be evidence of additional consideration in order to prevail on a contract theory. The intent is to obviate the problem that results when an express warranty is made. See *Hawkins v. McGee* (N.H.1929), where defendant doctor expressly promised to make patient's injured hand into a good or perfect hand and in fact made patient's hand worse. The doctor was liable in contract to the patient for the value of a good or perfect hand.

B. SPECIFIC PROCEDURES

An action in contract may also arise if a physician contracts with the patient to use a specific procedure and does not use that particular procedure or uses another which he has not contracted to perform.

In *Stewart v. Rudner* (Mich.1957) a woman explicitly contracted with her doctor to deliver her baby by Caesarean section, as she had had two previous stillbirths and feared for her own physical safety as well as that of her in-utero child. The plaintiff showed that every time the patient met with the doctor over the course of her pregnancy, her desire to have the Caesarean section performed was discussed. There was no dispute as to the existence of a contract. At the time of delivery; however, another physician was on duty and the child was delivered vaginally, and was stillborn. The original doctor with whom the agreement was made was held liable for breaching the contract for a specific procedure.

A cause of action for breach of contract may also arise from contracted non-medical duties as well as from the failure to render health care. For example, in *Chew v. Paul D. Meyer, M.D., P.A.* (Md.App. 1987), the patient's employer required all employees who missed work to produce a written explanation of their absence within fifteen days of the day missed. The patient underwent surgery and explained his employer's requirement to the doctor. The patient provided the doctor with his employer's forms to be completed to verify the reason for the patient's absence from work and stressed the importance of timely completion of the forms. The doctor failed to complete the forms, and the patient was fired. The court denied summary judgment, holding that a jury could find that the doctor had a contractual obligation to the patient. Furthermore, the jury could also find not only "contractual privity [but] that [such] privity would carry with it a concomitant tort duty."

C. CONTRACTS TO PERFORM SERVICES

When a patient and a doctor specifically contract that a particular physician will perform the contracted for services, and the physician does not do so, the patient may recover in a breach of contract action. In these actions, usually the doctor does not treat the patient and engages a substitute physician (or resident) to perform the services. In *Alexandridis v. Jewett* (1st Cir.1968), a woman contracted with a highly competent and experienced doctor to deliver her baby. The doctor and patient contracted that if this doctor was not available at the time of the patient's delivery, his equally qualified partner would perform the services required. The delivery, however, was performed by a first-year resident rather than the covering doctor. The patient, as a result of delivery, suffered rectal incontinence. The court held that even though the resident was not negligent, there was a breach of contract for which the plaintiff could recover. *Alexandridis* seems to hold that even if the delivery had been performed competently by a more qualified and experienced physician, the doctor with whom the patient had contracted would still be liable for a breach of contract, not for negligence. Once again, in order to successfully recover, the patient must prove by "clear proof" that there existed a specific contract with a physician for something more than professional services.

II. PRODUCT LIABILITY

Hospitals and physicians use and provide to patients products that are manufactured by others. The hospital's and physician's responsibilities attendant to the use of such products include using products correctly and warning patients about possible risks and side effects of the product selected.

In *Karibjanian v. Thomas Jefferson University Hospital* (E.D.Pa.1989), a widow alleged that her husband's death was caused by an injection of thorium dioxide administered by an agent of the defendant hospital. The widow alleged that the injection should not have been administered, that this product was inherently unsafe and that the defendant hospital knew or should have known it to be so. The widow's claim relied upon § 402A of the Restatement (Second) of Torts, which states in part:

(1) One who sells any product in a defective condition unreasonably dangerous to the user or consumer ... is subject to liability ... if (a) the

seller is engaged in the business of selling such a product. . . .

The defendant hospital contended that it was not in the "business of selling" thorium dioxide and instead, merely provided its services to the widow's decedent. The court held that as long as a hospital *regularly* supplies such a product to its patients, even if incidental to the services provided by the hospital, the hospital may be held liable under § 402A. The statute does not distinguish between a supplier of goods who also supplies services and a supplier who only supplies goods.

In most cases, prior to using or administering potentially dangerous products, a physician has a duty to warn patients about the risks and side effects associated with the product to be used. An example of the duty of the physician to warn patients about possible risks and side effects with regard to products manufactured by others is illustrated in *Tresemer v. Barke* (Cal.App.1978). In *Tresemer*, the plaintiff alleged that the defendant doctor breached his duty to warn her of the dangers of the Dalkon Shield when, subsequent to its insertion, the doctor obtained knowledge of the danger and did not notify the patient. As a general rule, a defendant owes a duty of care to all persons who are foreseeably endangered by his conduct. *Dillon v. Legg* (Cal.1968). The real question was whether it was the physician or the manufacturer who was responsible for providing the subsequent information to the patient. In assessing the manufacturer's liability, courts have consistently held that a manufacturer is not liable where the physician using the manufacturer's product has been made sufficiently aware of the risks associated with that product. *Wooten v. Johnson & Johnson Products, Inc.* (N.D.Ill.1986).

Tresemer states that the duty of the manufacturer to adequately warn is discharged by its warning of possible and actual dangers to the physicians as "it would be virtually impossible for a manufacturer to comply with the duty of direct warning, as there is no sure way to reach the patient." Once a physician is adequately informed by the manufacturer of the actual and possible dangers of a product, the physician "acts as a learned intermediary between the patient and the ... manufacturer, thus breaking the chain of liability." *Kirk v. Michael Reese Hospital and Medical Center* (Ill.1987)*; Vitanza v. The Upjohn Co.* (Conn.2001) (under the learned intermediary doctrine drug manufacturer has no duty to warn plaintiffs). The learned intermediary doctrine protects manufacturers from liability for failure to warn plaintiffs; however, it does not absolve manufactures from liability for failure to provide consumers with operating instructions. *Friedl v. Airsource* (Ill.App.2001). *Tresemer* holds that an action for failure to warn the patient may be maintained against the physician due to the continuing confidential relationship between the physician and patient, and that the danger arose from that relationship.

In general, physicians lack standing under consumer protection laws to sue manufacturers for concealing their products FDA approval status. *Balderston v. Medtronic Sofamor Danek, Inc.* (3rd Cir.2002). The plaintiff physician utilized the defendant's bone screws in numerous spinal fusion surgeries that he performed, believing that the screws had FDA approval. Upon discovering that the bone screws lacked FDA approval, the physician filed suit against the manufacturer. The Third Circuit reasoned that consumer protection laws provide a private right of action for a person who purchases goods or services primarily for private use and suffers a tangible loss. The court held that the plaintiff purchased the screws for business use and therefore could not invoke the consumer protection laws.

III. STRICT LIABILITY

Strict liability has yet to be applied to a physician with regard to his duties to a patient, although in scattered cases plaintiff have attempted to hold the physician liable on such a theory. In *Hoven v. Kelble* (Wis.1977), a plaintiff alleged strict liability against the defendant doctor on the basis that he was indeed a seller in the business of selling medical services and that the defective services rendered by defendant doctor were the cause of plaintiff's damages. *See Budding v. SSM Healthcare Sys.* (Mo. 2000) (hospital not held strictly liable for injuries resulting from defectively designed implants inserted at hospital); *Royer v. Catholic Med. Ctr.*, (N.H. 1999) (health care providers are not "sellers" of prosthetic devices and cannot be held strictly liable). Like *Karibjanian*, *Hoven* relies upon the Restatement (Second) of Torts § 402A to determine whether strict liability may be extended to the defendant for personal injuries occurring during the delivery of medical services. The *Hoven* court acknowledged that the § 402A strict liability test had not been applied beyond the sale of a defective and dangerous product; indeed, it had never been applied on the basis of medical services. The court did discuss the pros and cons of extending strict liability to the professional services of physicians. It reasoned that doctors contract with patients to provide treatment in a non-negligent manner, and that a patient cannot deem a doctor's treatment to be defective merely because he is not cured. Since the medical profession is not exact and a doctor is only required to provide treatment commensurate with the state of medical science, there is likely no social benefit in holding a physician strictly liable for injuries which may result from his professional practice. To hold a physician strictly liable may make doctors reluctant to treat patients with certain conditions.

Of course, the consumer of these services relies upon the skill and information of the physician, and the hospital and/or doctor is in a better position than the patient to ensure safe and effective treatment. Furthermore, the imposition of strict liability may be a strong deterrent to negligence as it encourages knowledge and safety. Nevertheless, the court concluded that society needs medical services and it is essential for these services to be readily available. The imposition of strict liability would likely increase the cost for those services and hinder much needed medical science advances. Having society's best interest and its need for medical services in mind, the court refused to impose strict liability upon physicians and hospitals under § 402A due to the "unknown costs and inability to assess the results" attendant with such an extension of the doctrine. The court noted, however, the ever-changing aspect of tort liability and recognized the possibility of applying strict liability in the future.

CHAPTER TEN

REFORMING THE LITIGATION SYSTEM

I. IN GENERAL: COST vs. QUALITY

Legislation and case law regarding the quality of and access to medical care may be more effective in addressing the medical malpractice crisis and reform of the litigation system than has previously been recognized. The primary objective of utilization review of health care resources and tort reform of malpractice litigation has been the containment of health care costs. As insurance premiums rise, higher costs are passed on to consumers. Additionally, the increase in malpractice litigation and the size of the awards has forced many physicians to practice "defensive medicine," i.e., excessive tests and procedures are ordered in an effort to avoid any possible oversight in the diagnosis and treatment of the patient. In response, health care insurers have instituted utilization review procedures in order to determine whether particular health care procedures should be "covered services" (i.e., paid for by the insurance carriers).

At the same time, licensing, accreditation, medical standards and other requirements for continuous quality improvement demand a certain level of care. These same standards are often used to determine the existence of a duty to the patient, as well as the level of care for evaluating a claim of negligence.

There are two competing and sometimes conflicting goals in the health care delivery system: cost containment (which limits the amount for resources utilized) and quality control (which demands a certain level of care, largely ignoring the cost). The tension between these goals results in the development of a standard of care that recognizes limited medical resources and limited insurance coverage along with a tort system that challenges the provider's professional judgment. The focus of tort reform has been to reduce the numbers of cases that require judicial resources (for example, by requiring pretrial screening panels and mandatory arbitration) and to limit the cost of malpractice awards (i.e. putting caps on recoveries). *See* Jonathan J. Frankel, Medical Malpractice Law and Health Care Cost Containment: Lessons For Reformers From The Clash of Cultures, 103 Yale L.J. 1297 (1994).

The challenge is evident: any effort at tort reform must consider the changing medical environment and the shared decision making authority that has emerged from changes in the health care delivery system. Specifically, physicians are no longer the sole managers of patient care. Physicians share this responsibility with hospital administrators, third party payers and ultimately utilization review boards. Changes in decision-making authority clearly has an impact on the nature of care provided, although the duty owed to the patient is not necessarily compromised. Indeed, many would argue that it is undesirable to modify the duty and/or standard of care legally required, since to do so would likely compromise patient welfare.

A. UTILIZATION REVIEW AND ACCESS TO CARE

Utilization review is a process used to determine whether certain care provided to a patient is medically necessary and thus reimbursable. Utilization review can be prospective or retrospective. The retrospective process, whereby the patient record is reviewed after the care has been provided is generally used pursuant to federally mandated guidelines for reimbursement under Medicare and for accreditation by the Joint Commission for Accreditation of Healthcare Organizations (JCAHO). Reimbursement to health care providers is often adjusted according to a certain rate, which is set in accordance with the standard applicable to the procedure. If the procedure is ultimately deemed unnecessary, reimbursement may be withheld entirely. The federal organizations, which review care to determine eligibility for coverage under Medicare and Medicaid, are the Quality Improvement Organizations (QIO), established pursuant to 42 U.S.C.A. § 1320c, et seq., Peer Review Improvement Act and its amendments.

Prospective utilization review calls for review of a case before care is given. The insurance company's utilization agent determines whether certain care is authorized as medically necessary and therefore will be reimbursed. This is a common reimbursement scheme used by health maintenance organizations. *See Wickline v. State of California* (Cal.App.1986).

In *Wickline*, a woman required vascular surgery to improve blood circulation in both of her legs. The state utilization organization, Medi–Cal, authorized ten days of in-patient care for the procedure. After surgery, the patient developed complications that required further hospitalization. In view of her "stormy" recovery, the surgeon requested an eight-day extension of her hospital stay beyond that already authorized by Medi–Cal. Medi–Cal approved only four days of the eight-day extension requested by the physician. The patient remained in the hospital for four days and was then discharged. At home, she developed severe complications including an infection at the surgical site and blood clots. The patient subsequently required amputation of her leg. After being re-hospitalized nine days after discharge, she alleged that her premature discharge caused the severity of the complications. According to her complaint, if she had been permitted to remain in the hospital, the complications would have been detected earlier in time to save her leg.

The California Court of Appeals declined to find liability on behalf of Medi–Cal because there was no evidence that the physician exhausted his option to keep the patient hospitalized. The physician did not re-contact Medi–Cal at the end of four days to request continued care for the patient. Nevertheless, the court did establish that an organization performing utilization review owes a duty of care to the patient. The court held that a "patient who requires treatment and who is harmed when care which should be provided is not provided should recover for the injuries suffered from all those responsible for the deprivation of such care, including, when appropriate, health care payers." Unreasonable disregard of *appeals* of non-coverage decisions may qualify as an "appropriate trigger of liability."

The standard applied in *Wickline* may differ in the private insurance sector where the duty of care is governed by the insurance contract. Nevertheless, if the contract establishes a duty, utilization review decisions can trigger liability if they result in injury to a patient. In *Wilson v. Blue Cross of So. California* (Cal.App.1990), a psychiatric patient committed suicide after being discharged from a hospital. The agent responsible for the utilization review decisions refused to authorize additional in-patient treatment, even though the treating physician requested 3–4 weeks of further hospital care. The court limited the holding of Wickline, but expanded the potential liability of outside reviewers by determining that the utilization review board could be held at least partially liable if its determination was negligent and was a substantial factor in bringing about the suicide.

Corcoran v. United Healthcare, Inc. (5th Cir.1992) also recognized that utilization review decisions substantially affect treatment decisions, as patients are likely to choose that which is authorized or covered by the plan. In *Corcoran*, a pregnant woman agreed to be discharged to home nursing when her HMO would not authorize in-patient coverage. She ultimately lost her 32–week fetus that went into fetal distress during the absence of the nurse. No actual determination about liability was made. It was determined, however, that the Employee Retirement Income Security Act of 1974 (ERISA) preempted the claim. *See* Peter H. Mihaly, Health Care Utilization Review: Potential Exposures to Negligence Liability, 52 Ohio St. L.J. 1289 (1991).

B.   PEER REVIEW AND MEDICAL MALPRACTICE LITIGATION

Efforts of the medical community to improve the quality and delivery of health care have resulted in both voluntary and statutorily mandated review of services by means of peer review or quality assessment procedures. As a consequence, the issue has arisen as to the discoverability of information compiled by peer review committees in the course of their proceedings. Typically, such discovery is sought by a medical malpractice plaintiff, who seeks to determine whether a hospital knew that its physician was not competent to perform a certain procedure, or whether a subsequent inquiry into the particular incident yielded any significant (or helpful) findings.

Most recent cases recognize the confidentiality of certain peer review materials. However, any immunity from discovery is likely to depend upon the type of peer review organization or quality assurance committee that has generated the information. A quality improvement organizations (QIO) reviews care for eligibility under federal reimbursement programs such as Medicare. A utilization review committee, in contrast, performs a broader function. Typically, it is a committee that is created to determine necessity of care (and thus coverage). Utilization review is now common in state and private insurance programs. A type of "peer review" may also be performed by those committees which evaluate quality assurance, "continuous quality improvement," staff credentials and similar programs. See *Todd v. South Jersey Hospital System* (D.N.J.1993). Whether the documents generated by such "peer review" groups are protected from discovery is dependent upon both the type of committee that generates the information and any statutory provisions concerning confidentiality. In *Franzon v. Massena Mem'l Hosp.* (N.D.N.Y.1999), the court held that the plaintiff's interest in the privileged physician peer review and quality assurance materials outweighed the protected interest of confidentiality. Denying access to that information could prevent plaintiff from bringing his action altogether against the Hospital and various hospital officials.

The Quality Improvement Organization Act provides federal protection of confidentiality of documents for QIOs. A leading judicial decision in this area is *General Care Corp. v. Mid–South Foundation for Medical Care, Inc.* (W.D.Tenn.1991). The court held that information compiled by a PRO is presumed to be confidential and thus the hospital was not required to disclose it. *Todd*, supra, supported this decision, holding that the Quality Improvement Organization Act protected from discovery documents that were collected and generated by the QIO while performing its statutorily defined functions. Nevertheless, *Todd* also qualified its holding by stating that these same documents would be discoverable if they could be independently obtained from another committee or department. See *Todd*.

In *Chandra v. Sprinkle* (Mo.1984), by contrast, a Missouri court held that no peer review privilege existed to protect the discovery of factual information compiled by an "Ad Hoc Committee" which was appointed by the hospital to investigate the care of an infant who suffered respiratory arrest. The court refused to recognize any self-evaluation privilege in the absence of a statute, and issued an order compelling discovery, despite public policy concerns that confidentiality of such documents is necessary to maintain an effective evaluation program. In contrast to *Chandra,* most courts do hold that peer review documents should be protected from discovery, particularly, if so ordered by statute. *See Dallas County Med. Soc'y v. Ubinas–Brache* (Tex.App.2001); *Morse v. Gerity* (D.Conn.1981). Whether the privilege applies is often clear from the facts of the case; however, in cases where the issue is disputed it is a matter for the trial judge. Miller

v. Milton Hosp. and Medical Center, Inc. (Mass.App. 2002).

State statute predominately governs the protection of documents generated by utilization review committees and other such groups. Virtually all such statutes provide protection of committee members from personal liability for their good faith participation as peer review members. Such protection is not necessarily provided however, for information generated by other types of groups. This varies among states, and is governed by local statute. According to the Health Care Peer Review Act of 1992, the confidentiality right protects peer review records from being obtained through discovery.

In those cases where peer review or quality control groups are not covered by statute, a state may recognize such protection as a "critical self-analysis" privilege at common law. "The purpose of this privilege is to encourage self-evaluation and the benefits that may flow there from, and to avoid the chilling effect upon such self-analysis which would result from complete disclosure." *Todd*. Such privileges are generally not absolute and can be overridden by a showing that the need for production of documents outweighs the public interest in confidentiality. Usually, a court will balance the availability of the information from other sources, the harm that non-disclosure will cause, and any possible prejudice to the organization's investigation. In *Todd*, the court held that the patient's need for information regarding alleged negligent obstetrical care was sufficient to overcome the critical self-analysis privilege. Consequently, it ordered production of certain quality assurance documents, even though materials generated specifically for "Utilization Review" were protected by statute and not subject to discovery.

Such privileges from discovery recognize the inherent conflict between improving quality of care by candid review procedures and assisting an injured plaintiff in proving his claim of negligence. The goal of minimizing costs of health care litigation may eventually affect the discoverability of opinions or reports prepared by peer review or utilization review organizations.

II. ACCESSIBILITY, QUALITY, AND AFFORDABILITY

Reform of the litigation system that began in earnest in the 1990s attempted to address several concerns: accessibility of services, quality of care and affordability. Accessibility becomes an issue when escalating costs of malpractice liability insurance drives physicians out of certain practice areas. Quality of care suffers when physicians, forced to practice defensive medicine, have limited overall resources and must struggle to provide adequate care. Finally, escalating costs of health care are inevitably passed on to consumers and further diminish the affordability of healthcare.

Reform of the litigation system has taken the form of encouraging alternative dispute resolution including arbitration, mediation and early settlement, as well as the screening of spurious claims. A number of states have imposed limitations on contingent fee arrangements between the attorney and client so that more of the award goes to the injured plaintiff. Some states have eliminated the collateral source rule which otherwise precludes the plaintiff from recovering from both the tortfeasor and a collateral source, such as insurance. Some jurisdictions now permit allocation of liability among tortfeasors and may allow claims under theories such as enterprise liability. A number of jurisdictions have imposed limitations on the total amount of damages that can be awarded. Some have attempted to abolish joint and several liability. Some states have reduced litigation by shortening the applicable statute of limitations for medical malpractice claims. *See* Marshall B. Kapp, Medical Malpractice Reform as Part of Health Care Reform, 1994 Version, 68 FLBJ 28 (May 1994). Most of these legislative efforts have survived constitutional challenges.

Another difficulty with reforming the tort system for medical injuries is that there is little agreement as to how to evaluate the success of various measures. The only consensus has been that statutory limitations on damages have been effective, assuming, of course, that effectiveness is measured by a reduction in the frequency and severity of claims, and by lower insurance premiums. *Kapp,* supra.

A. AVAILABILITY OF MALPRACTICE INSURANCE

The initial concern about the large number of malpractice claims and the size of the awards was that it would affect the availability of medical care by forcing physicians to practice defensive medicine. Another major concern has been the effect of such awards on the availability of affordable malpractice insurance to health care professionals, particularly the physician. As successful claims increased, many malpractice insurers suffered severe losses and either withdrew from the market or increased their premiums dramatically. *See Meier v. Anderson* (E.D.Pa.1988). Many states responded with the legislative efforts discussed earlier aimed at limiting or reallocating such losses.

The medical community (and others to whom the losses have shifted) has also responded. One approach has been to attack the legislation on constitutional grounds. In *Meier,* a physician challenged the Pennsylvania tort reform scheme, which both limited the liability of the insurer and reallocated the losses. Specifically, the act required health care providers to contribute to a fund from which victims of malpractice could collect their awards if the awards were in excess of the limits of the insurance to ensure that they received adequate compensation. The Act was constitutionally challenged on the basis that the right to practice one's profession is protected by both the due process and the equal protection clause of the fourteenth amendment. Such legislation was alleged to have potential economic effects on that right. The court held that the right at issue was not a fundamental right "explicitly or implicitly guaranteed by the Constitution," and therefore not worthy of special protection.

Therefore, any challenge to the law would be subject to the rational basis standard, and the law would stand if there was a rational basis for concluding that the law serves a legitimate governmental interest. In denying that the law was unconstitutional, the court noted that "states have a legitimate interest in regulating the practice of medicine" and to assure the availability of medical malpractice insurance, and can enact nonarbitrary legislation to that end without violating substantive due process. *See Meier,* supra.

The *Meier* court also rejected the defendant's equal protection challenge alleging that the Act was under-inclusive as it targeted only medical doctors and not other professionals such as chiropractors. It also rejected the argument that law was over-inclusive as it required all doctors to pay into the fund regardless of their past claims history. These provisions were held to be rationally related to the goals of the Act, which was to increase the availability of malpractice insurance. The "rational basis" standard makes it difficult to challenge such legislation on constitutional grounds.

B. INSURER'S DUTY TO DEFEND AND INDEMNIFY AND SETTLE

The insurer's duty to defend, indemnify and even settle (if practical) is important, both to the interests of the professional who may be liable for a substantial award, and to the injured party, who seeks just and timely compensation. The obligation of an insurer to defend its insured is broader than the duty of indemnity.

In *Snyder v. National Union Fire Insurance Co.* (S.D.N.Y.1988), a New York District Court held that to trigger the duty to defend, the "plaintiff need merely to show that her complaint brings the claim within the coverage of the policy." The pleadings must allege actions and injury that are within the terms of the policy. The duty to defend arises whether or not ultimate liability will be proved. A North Carolina court referred to this as the "comparison test", which involves comparing the allegations of the complaint side-by-side with the particular terms of the policy to determine if the duty to defend arises. If the duty to defend arises, then the insurance company is obligated to provide a defense regardless of the ultimate disposition of the case. *See St. Paul Fire and Marine Ins. Co. v. Vigilant Ins. Co.* (M.D.N.C.1989). In *St. Paul*, a duty to defend was held to exist even though a second insurance company had assumed coverage during the latter part of the doctor-patient relationship.

In *Snyder*, the plaintiff alleged both civil liability for malpractice and criminal liability for assault and sexual abuse. The issue arose as to whether the insurer's duty to defend was negated by the criminal allegations (and ultimate conviction of the physician) as the policy contained an exclusion of coverage for injury resulting from criminal acts. The court held that in order for an insurance company to avoid an obligation to defend, it must show the allegations are *entirely* within the exclusions of the policy. *See Snyder*, supra.

Indemnification raises different issues. Whether the insurer must pay on a claim will depend upon the liability of the insured and, if an exclusion applies, upon whether the findings by the court bring the case within that policy's exclusion. In *Snyder,* the plaintiff was required to show both (a) that there was no intent to cause injury and (b) that the injury did not arise from the criminal acts of alleged sexual abuse. If the injury did result from criminal acts, the insurer would be entitled to disclaim coverage under the policy.

Whether an insurance company defends or settles claims against its insured, it owes "a duty to act in good faith and without negligence." *Insurance Company of North America v. Medical Protective Co.* (10th Cir.1985). In *Brown v. Guarantee Ins. Co.* (Cal.App.1957), the appellate court suggested several factors that would aid in a determination of "bad faith" These include:

"1) the strength of the insured claimant's case on the issue of liability and damages; 2) attempts by the insurer to induce the insured to contribute to a settlement; 3) failure of the insurer to properly investigate the circumstances so as to ascertain the evidence against the insured; 4) the insurer's rejection of advice of its own attorney or agent; 5) failure of the insurer to inform the insured of a compromise offer; 6) the amount of financial risk to which each party is exposed in the event of a refusal to settle; 7) the fault of the insured in inducing the insurer's rejection of a compromise offer by misleading it as to the facts; and 8) any other factors tending to establish or negate bad faith on the part of the insurer." *Brown v. Guarantee Ins. Co.* (Cal.App.1957).

The insurer also has a duty to keep the physician informed of all settlement negotiations, and to act in good faith, without negligence in efforts to effect a settlement. This duty remains in effect whether or not the insured is willing to consent to any settlement.

C.   SCREENING OF SPURIOUS CLAIMS

Another legislative response to the rising number of malpractice claims has been the establishment of mechanisms for screening spurious claims. The goal of such legislation is to increase the availability of malpractice insurance and health care by discouraging unwarranted claims, and to avoid the expense of frivolous litigation, which wastes judicial and medical resources. This type of legislation is frequently challenged constitutionally, on the basis that it violates equal protection and due process of law, and/or that it interferes with access to the court system and the right of trial by jury. As new legislation is being tailored to address these concerns, and as courts primarily have employed a "rational basis" level of review when evaluating these claims, the majority of the legislative reforms have been able to withstand constitutional scrutiny. Specifically, most measures have been found to be rationally or reasonably related to the goals of reducing the costs associated with large numbers of medical malpractice claims.

Whether a particular legislative scheme will survive a constitutional challenge depends upon the method of screening, and the effect of the screen, (i.e., under what conditions a plaintiff may gain access to the courts after being "screened out" on a claim that was held to lack merit). See Keyes v. Humana Hospital Alaska, Inc. (Alaska 1988). The types of screening measures vary among jurisdictions. Some states require that prior to litigation being commenced, a mediation process be made available to the litigants. Other states require screening of all claims prior to litigation by an expert panel or a judicial tribunal. The findings of such a panel or tribunal are used to evaluate the merit of the case, and may be admissible in the subsequent litigation. See Blood v. Lea (Mass.1988); Aldana v. Holub (Fla.1980).

Constitutional challenges alleging that the screening process violates equal protection have been based primarily on the premise that the malpractice litigant is treated differently from other tort litigants. For example, the screening process requires a malpractice claimant to undergo an additional step in the judicial process not required of other tort litigants. Once again, since the malpractice litigant does not belong to a suspect class in need of any special protection, there only need be a rational basis for the legislation. Today, most screening mechanisms generally survive the equal protection arguments. *See Keyes*, supra.

Screening legislation has also been challenged on due process grounds. The typical argument is that such screening mechanisms violate the plaintiff's right to access to the courts and potentially the right to trial by jury, particularly if the screen is mandatory. The level of due process protection afforded to the plaintiff for access to the courts depends upon the substantive claim. Again, no special due process protection is afforded to malpractice litigants since the right they assert is not entitled to special protection. Absent the claim of a fundamental right, courts have held that access to the courts may be delayed, as long as there is a rational basis for doing so. Reducing unnecessary costs of malpractice litigation has been held to constitute a rational reason for delay. *Keyes*, supra.

Yet another avenue for objection on constitutional grounds is the argument that the plaintiff's right to trial by jury is denied by the decision-making authority of screening tribunals. Courts have held that where the opinion of the review panel serves merely as evidence or as a "rebuttable presumption" in the jury trial which follows, the plaintiff's right is not compromised. In such a case, the same evidence and arguments may be presented to the jury to rebut the panel's opinion. On the other hand, screening mechanisms that give the panels original jurisdiction to assess liability and/or damages, or that serve as the sole basis for judgment are more likely to be successfully challenged. *Fein-*

stein v. Massachusetts General Hosp. (D.Mass.1979); *Keyes*, supra. Finally, there are cases where repeated delays in convening the screening tribunal make the right to trial by jury difficult to exercise. *Keyes*. In *Keyes*, the court found that the maximum possible delay was eighty days, and held that the right to trial by jury was not unreasonably compromised .

Objections to medical review panels or screening tribunals based upon substantive due process grounds have been uniformly rejected. The Keyes court specifically found "[t]he review procedure to be a reasonable legislative response to a perceived crisis in medical malpractice insurance rates, a means of assuring the availability of malpractice insurance coverage at reasonable rates and of improving the availability and reducing the cost of medical care in general, by attempting to eliminate frivolous malpractice claims and encourage settlement of meritorious ones." See *Keyes*, supra.

Procedural due process safeguards are also not compromised if the litigant is provided a full opportunity to present his case at trial. Procedural due process is protected where the decisions of the screening panels or tribunals are subject to appeal. The function of such review panels is generally to evaluate the claim to determine whether there is sufficient evidence to raise a legitimate question of liability. It has been held that the tribunal should use the same standard as a judge would use in ruling on a motion for directed verdict. Thus the function of the tribunal is to evaluate the sufficiency, not the weight, of the evidence. See *Blood v. Lea* (Mass.1988). Typically state screening requirements are also applicable in federal courts in diversity actions. See *Feinstein*; *Woods v. Holy Cross Hospital* (5th Cir.1979). The federal court in *Seck by Seck v. Hamrang* (S.D.N.Y.1987), however, held to the contrary on the basis that the screening process amounted to a pretrial procedure not required in a federal court. *Seck by Seck* commented that to require compliance with the screening mechanisms of the state would conflict with the broad procedural powers of federal courts.

While most state screening procedures have been carefully tailored to avoid constitutional infirmity, some constitutional challenges have been successful. In *Aldana v. Holub* (Fla.1980), the Florida mediation procedure included a mandatory ten-month limitation period. The statutory scheme further provided that if the mediation was not completed within the ten month period, for *any* reason, (including unavailability of space on court dockets), the right was denied. The court held that the legislative scheme violated due process in that its rigid requirements concerning the time limits were arbitrary and capricious. The court commented that allowing extensions to the time limits would not correct the constitutional problem since the law itself amounted to a denial of access to the courts.

An alternative to screening panels used in some courts is a "certificate of merit" requirement. Such legislation typically requires that the plaintiff's attorney certify that he has consulted with a knowledgeable health professional in the same specialty as the defendant who has reviewed the case and issued a written report. The plaintiff's attorney certifies that the health professional concludes that there are reasonable grounds for filing the action, and the report is filed with an affidavit or certification. See e.g. New Jersey Stat. Ann. § 2A:53A–26 (2002); *Chamberlain v. Giampapa* (3d Cir.2000). Some courts have held such legislation to be constitutional, while others have held that it unconstitutionally delegates judicial power to non-judicial persons, in derogation of separation of powers doctrine.

III. CHANGING THE LITIGATION SYSTEM

A. ARBITRATION

Another avenue for deterring litigation is to agree to a form of dispute resolution at the time that the professional relationship begins, and prior to treatment. Alternatively, the decision to arbitrate may be made voluntarily by both parties at the time of litigation. In *Morris v. Metriyakool* (Mich.1984), an arbitration provision was contained in the hospital's admission form at the time that the plaintiff entered the hospital. The form complied with Michigan law requiring that the option be stated on the form in large, boldface type immediately above the patient's signature. It had to be clear that the arbitration provision was optional, and further, it had to be freely revocable by the patient within sixty (60) days after discharge. The court held that the Michigan law that provided arbitration by a three-member panel "did not deprive patients of a fair and impartial decision maker in violation of their due process rights." Furthermore, the court held that such agreements did not constitute contracts of adhesion.

Houk v. Furman (D.Me.1985) concerned the constitutionality of yet another legislative scheme: Maine's requirement that the plaintiff submit a 90–day "pre-litigation notice" intended to encourage settlement or non-judicial resolution of malpractice actions. The court held that the statute did not violate equal protection or due process protections, even though non-compliance with the statute resulted in denial of recovery. The court also held that the notice provision applied in federal court diversity actions as well as in state claims. Using the "rational basis" standard of review, *Houk* held that the Maine law had a rational relationship to the purpose of encouraging settlement of claims and of disposing of lawsuits through alternative dispute resolution. The court also found that although non-compliance could bar recovery, it was held to not unduly burdensome such that it would offend due process requirements.

B.   CAPS ON MALPRACTICE AWARDS

Another legislative tool used to respond to the large number of malpractice cases and the rise in health care costs is statutory caps on damages awarded by the courts. In some cases overall caps are imposed; in others only certain types of damages (such as no economic loss/recovery) are limited. In other cases the law allows such mechanisms as installment payments on future damages to regulate the manner in which damages are paid. In *Etheridge v. Medical Center Hospitals* (Va.1989), the jury returned a verdict in the amount of $2,750,000.00 against two defendants whose negligence resulted in brain damage and paralysis of the plaintiff. In accordance with Virginia's statutory recovery limit, the trial court reduced the verdict to $750,000.00. The plaintiff challenged the constitutionality of the statute alleging privacy violations on the basis that the statutory cap "preordains the result of the hearing." She also alleged that the statute violated equal protection of the laws on the basis that malpractice plaintiffs are treated differently from other tort victims. Finally, she alleged that the statute violated the constitutional mandate of separation of powers, claiming that legislative caps serve to interfere "with the power of the court to enforce its own judgments." The court rejected all of the constitutional claims and held that the statutory scheme was a reasonable exercise of legitimate goals. *See also St. Mary's Hospital, Inc. v. Phillipe* (Fla.2000).

Once again, as malpractice litigants are not designated as a suspect class and no fundamental right has been identified regarding these claims, the courts on both the federal and state level generally apply a "rational basis" level of review. In most cases the courts are able to identify a reasonable basis for the legislature to conclude that imposing caps on damage awards promotes the legitimate state objective of reducing the cost of malpractice. The caps on malpractice awards appear to be applicable in both state and federal actions. *See Hoffman v. United States* (9th Cir.1985); *Adams v. Children's Mercy Hospital* (Mo.1992); *Keeton v. Mansfield Obstetrics and Gynecology Assoc., Inc.* (N.D.Ohio 1981).

Limitations on damage awards have also been claimed to compromise the plaintiff's right to trial by jury. This approach has also not been very successful. As explained by the court in *Adams v. Childrens Mercy Hospital* (Mo.1992), the jury has no substantive right to determine damages. While the primary role of the jury is fact-finding, it need not include an assessment of damages. It is the function of the court to apply the substantive law to the fact finding process and that may legitimately include the application of damage limitations. *See Adams*. Thus it has been held that the role of the jury is to determine or assess the damages, but not to dictate the consequences of that determination. See *Etheridge v. Medical Center Hospitals* (Va. 1989).

The reasoning in *Etheridge* and similar opinions was criticized in *Keeton v. Mansfield Obstetrics and Gynecology Assoc., Inc.* (N.D.Ohio 1981). *Keeton* questioned the rationale that controlling the cost of malpractice insurance would promote the availability of health care services. The court in *Keeton* held that the legislative goal was to shift the risk of medical malpractice from the provider to the patient (who is least able to afford it) by limiting the patient's ability to obtain full compensation for the negligence. *Keeton* agreed, however, that the measures were not unconstitutional.

"Although this Court has very seriously questioned the reasoning behind this legislation and is very dissatisfied with its effect (placing the burden of paying for the negligence of health care providers on those least able to afford it—the seriously injured plaintiff), the Court also recognizes that its only function is to determine whether the challenged legislation is a reasonable exertion of governmental authority or whether the legislation is shown to be arbitrary and capricious."

C. CAPS ON ATTORNEY'S FEES

As an alternative to limiting the amount of awards in malpractice claims, some legislation limits the amount of the legal fee that the attorney may receive pursuant to a contingency fee agreement. Such limitations have also not been found to violate equal protection, due process, or the separation of powers doctrine. See *Roa v. Lodi Medical Group, Inc.* (Cal.1985). In *Roa*, a due process violation was claimed on the basis that the limitation interfered with the plaintiff's right to obtain counsel. The plaintiff argued that if fees were too low, it might be impossible to obtain counsel at all, and that less incentive would exist for an attorney to pursue additional damages. The court rejected this argument, citing a long history of cases establishing the validity of regulating attorney fees. Indeed, limitation of fees may prevent attorneys from fabricating unjust claims in order to collect exorbitant fees. In addition, limitations may protect legitimate plaintiffs from extortion by unscrupulous attorneys.

Roa also contained a strong dissenting opinion. Three of the judges claimed that the limitation of fees would permit defendants to pay any rate for counsel, while plaintiffs could not even pay the fair market rate. Accordingly, the dissent opined that this would make it difficult for plaintiffs to obtain competent legal representation, which is a constitutional guarantee.

Another issue is whether caps on attorney's fees set by state law would apply to federal claims under the Federal Torts Claim Act (FTCA). In *Jackson v. United States* (9th Cir.1989), the court held that state law would apply to the extent necessary to establish the substantive liability of the government. Finding a conflict between the limits set by state law and those in the FTCA, the court held that the amount of the attorney's fees had no relationship to the substantive law. Thus, the FTCA preempted state law with respect to the issue of attorney's fees.

D. STATUTORY RATE FREEZE ON MALPRACTICE PREMIUMS

A final method of addressing the malpractice insurance crisis has been through direct control or restriction of rate increases on malpractice premiums. In *Medical Malpractice Joint Underwriting Association of Rhode Island v. Paradis* (D.R.I.1991), the federal district court held that such restrictions on rate increases violate the "takings clause" of the fifth amendment on the basis that property of the insurance industry was taken without just compensation. Evidence of this taking was held to be in terms of the accrued deficit that the underwriting fund would incur. Furthermore, the court found that the recoupment methods outlined by the legislature did not allow adequate compensation for the insurers. Thus, at least in that case, the legislative freeze on insurance rates carried the concept of "reform" too far and was held to be unconstitutional.

IV. COUNTERSUITS

In medical malpractice litigation, the countersuit is an action brought by the physician against the patient who previously brought a malpractice suit. The countersuit typically alleges that the malpractice action was brought in bad faith upon a claim that lacked merit, and the physician seeks damages for malicious prosecution, abuse of process or a similar claim. In *Morowitz v. Marvel* (D.C.App. 1980), two physicians filed suit to collect medical fees owed to them. The patient filed a countersuit alleging medical malpractice, but subsequently withdrew the complaint. The court held that although abuse of the legal system is certainly disfavored, would-be litigants with meritorious claims must be provided with free access to the court system. The court held that in order for the physicians to prevail on a claim of malicious prosecution, four separate elements must be pled and proven: (1) The underlying suit was decided in the physician's favor; (2) the defendant showed malice; (3) there was no probable cause for the underlying suit; and (4) "special damages" were suffered by the plaintiff as a result of the original suit. Special damages are those beyond which would necessarily be expected by anyone involved in a lawsuit. Thus even "professional defamatory type" damages must be expected in this type of suit, and therefore do not qualify as "special damages." Although most jurisdictions do not require "special damages" claims for malicious prosecution have traditionally been difficult to establish.

A second important issue addressed in *Morowitz* is whether a suit for malicious prosecution may be brought against the attorney who initiates the allegedly frivolous action. California specifically rejects the idea that counsel would be liable. There is no privity of contract and the attorney is not an intended beneficiary. Furthermore, the court identified obvious public policy concerns. An Illinois appellate court, also rejecting a countersuit against the attorney, commented that to do so would create an "insurmountable conflict of interest between the attorney and client." *Berlin v. Nathan* (Ill.App. 1978). Finally, New York reached the same conclusion on the basis that "[w]hatever may be the constraints imposed by the Code of Professional Responsibility with the associated sanctions of professional discipline when baseless legal proceedings are instituted by a lawyer on behalf of a client, the courts have not recognized any liability of the lawyer to third parties ..." *Drago v. Buonagurio* (N.Y.Ct.App.1978).

Countersuits raise an interesting dilemma. What if a physician, wary of a malpractice action, waits for the tort statute of limitation to expire before filing suit for an unpaid fee? The contract statute of limitation is generally longer than the tort statute, so a collection action may be instituted without fear of triggering a malpractice counterclaim. Three possibilities exist: (1) the collection action could go forward as intended with the malpractice action barred by the statute of limitations; (2) the malpractice action could proceed on the basis that instituting the contract claim implicitly waived the tort statute; or (3) the malpractice action would be precluded, except that poor delivery of medical care could still be a defense to an action seeking to recover the physicians' fee.

CHAPTER ELEVEN

NEW MEDICAL TECHNOLOGY

I. INTELLECTUAL PROPERTY

As medical technology ventures further into uncharted territory, the law is forced to keep pace with the medical procedures, devices and equipment being developed. Even before issues of misuse and negligence arise, the new technology itself presents a myriad of legal issues. Can the new invention or technique be "owned" and, if so, who "owns" it? Can the invention be patented? Would the owner be liable if the invention or technique causes harm or is produced in a defective manner? Does the owner have a "duty to warn" of possible harm? What is the obligation of the clinician who uses the device, procedure, or technique? And if there is liability, what kind of damages will be awarded? These are only some of the questions that will need to be addressed regarding the intersection of medical technology, intellectual property and the law.

Intellectual property is material such as ideas, discoveries, and inventions which can be protected under federal law. Until recently, the United States Patent and Trademark Office ("PTO") rarely issued patents for medical devices, surgical equipment, or drugs. Advances in medical technology in recent years, however, have spurred PTO to grant patents for some of these types of inventions.

Learned Intermediary Doctrine

In *Vitanza v. Upjohn* (2d Cir.2000), the Second Circuit Court of Appeals considered whether a pharmaceutical company should be insulated from product liability pursuant to the legal principle known as the "learned intermediary" doctrine. According to this common law doctrine, a manufacturer does not have a duty to warn individual patients who use its drugs if the manufacturer adequately informed the prescribing physician of the possible risks associated with the drug's use. The duty to warn the patient of possible risks would then fall on the prescribing physician. The doctrine applies specifically to medical devices and pharmaceuticals that are inherently "unavoidably unsafe products" and by law, must be prescribed or distributed by a physician as a "learned intermediary" between the manufacturer and consumer of its product. In *Vitanza,* a drug manufacturer gave free samples of a drug to a physician and the physician, in turn, provided the sample to a patient. The patient's spouse subsequently used the sample and later died from an allergic reaction to the drug. The Second Circuit affirmed the district court's grant of summary judgment in favor of the manufacturer, maintaining that learned intermediary doctrine was applicable and thereby shielded the manufacturer from liability.

There are some circumstances in which the learned intermediary doctrine will not apply. If a court finds that the manufacturer marketed the product directly to the public, the doctrine may not provide a defense. In *Perez v. Wyeth Labs.* (N.J. 1999), the New Jersey Supreme Court held that state's learned intermediary doctrine did not apply when a pharmaceutical company used direct-to-consumer advertising to market a new drug to the public. The court explained that the doctrine has diminished utility when a manufacturer targets its advertising to consumers, rather than physicians. The court also noted that the Food and Drug Administration (FDA) requires drug advertisers to warn consumers about risks associated with the drug's use and that a consumer should be able to rely on the accuracy and comprehensiveness of those warnings. The court remanded the case to determine whether the manufacturer complied with the advertising regulations set forth by FDA, and if not, whether any violation of the regulations was the proximate cause of the plaintiff's injuries.

Physician's Liability

In 1994, the American Medical Association (AMA) prohibited the practice of patenting medical devices, surgical equipment and drugs. The AMA viewed the patenting of medical products as unethical and feared that such a trend might compromise the physician's ethical obligations to patient care. The landmark case of Pallin v. Singer (D.Vt.1995), however, led the AMA to change its position. In *Pallin*, the plaintiff physician alleged that the defendants were infringing on a patented surgical technique developed by plaintiff for use during cataract surgery. In declining to grant the defendant's Motion for Summary Judgment, the court maintained that there were genuine issues of material fact concerning the patent's validity. *Pallin* became the first case of alleged patent infringement for medical products and it set the trend for future issues in the medical product arena.

Physicians routinely prescribe new drugs or utilize medical devices (i.e. prosthetics) for patient use. If the medical product used is defective and the patient suffers injury, physicians may be held liable. Such liability generally depends upon a finding of negligence in the prescription, use, or application of the device. The question of whether a physician might, under some circumstances, be held strictly liable as a guarantor of a defective product is more difficult to answer. Cases of this type usually trigger issues of informed consent.

New and Experimental Products

Physicians generally avoid liability for using new drug products as long as the decision and manner of prescription is not negligent and the patient's informed consent is secured. If experimental drugs are used, the experimental protocol must be carefully observed and informed consent specific to the experimental product must be obtained. The informed consent protocol is far more extensive than in ordinary medical procedures. In *Kernke v. Menninger Clinic, Inc.* (D.Kan.2001), the court declined to grant summary judgment to several defendant physicians on a claim of medical malpractice when the physicians enrolled a schizophrenic patient in a study monitoring the effects of an investigational new drug. The patient became more depressed and psychotic after taking the experimental drug, subsequently escaped from the clinic, and was found dead approximately three months later. Relatives of the patient alleged malpractice on the grounds that included lack of informed consent, misrepresentation of the possible benefits of the patient's enrollment in the study, and failure of the clinic to establish proper security measures. The court held that there were genuine issues of material fact as to whether the physicians breached their duty of care to the patient and whether this breach was the proximate cause of the patient's death.

Physicians are urged to document patient concerns prior to seeking informed consent. Physicians involved in experimental trials with drugs or devices should also be advised that they can contact the Food and Drug Administration (FDA) if they have additional questions or concerns. While these steps may not insulate the physician from liability, they are an important protective measure if suit is ultimately filed.

Informed Consent

Physicians can be held liable for performing a procedure or otherwise treating a patient without the patient's informed consent. In the landmark California decision of *Cobbs v. Grant* (Cal.1972), it was held that the physician has a duty to provide the patient with as much information as is material and necessary to make the decision of whether to undergo the treatment. Such information includes a description of available treatment options and the risks associated with each. In *Moore v. Regents of the Univ. of California* (Cal.1990), the Supreme Court of California concluded that a physician must also inform a patient of any economic or personal interests that could affect the physician's recommended course of treatment in order for the patient's consent to be valid. In *Moore*, the plaintiff underwent a surgical procedure to treat a form of leukemia. His physicians did not advise him that the tissue and cells removed would be used in their research efforts or that the tissue had potential commercial value. After establishing a cell line from plaintiff's tissue, the physicians applied for a patent and listed themselves as inventors who would ultimately share in the profits as paid consultants. They included the attending physician and researcher at the hospital owned and operated by the defendant, Regents of the University of California. The plaintiff was never advised or consulted about the research or his participation.

In the litigation that followed, the court concluded that the plaintiff had causes of action against the defendant physician for breach of fiduciary duty to the plaintiff arising out of his failure to disclose his research and economic interests in plaintiff's cells. They also failed to obtain informed consent prior to extraction of the cells. The court held that a reasonable patient would want to know whether his physician had an economic interest or profit motive that might affect his recommended treatment. Although the law does not prohibit a physician from conducting research in the same field in which he practices, it does recognize that a physician with a research interest in his patient has potentially conflicting loyalties. The court concluded that the cause of action for violating this legally protected interest could either be characterized as a breach of a fiduciary duty to disclose all facts necessary to secure consent, or performance of a medical procedure without informed consent.

II. TELEMEDICINE

A. GENERALLY

Telemedicine is the use of telecommunications and information technologies to provide clinical care to individuals at distant sites and to transmit diagnostic and treatment information necessary to provide that care. This information may be communicated in various forms including audio-visual conferencing and e-mail. It may include medical images, the patient's medical record, and even output data from diagnostic or monitoring devices. Telemedicine allows one healthcare provider to support or consult with another healthcare provider who may be geographically and technologically at a remote location. Initially telemedicine was an expensive boutique alternative for practitioners in distant practice areas to seek the assistance of specialists in urban medical centers. Thus clinicians in rural areas far removed from medical centers with the most advanced technology could access a full range of specialists and sophisticated treatment options without having to travel long distances. Today, however, telemedicine has rapidly become an integral part of modern health care delivery. The previously high-priced, government-sponsored demonstration projects are now routinely linking academic medical centers to primary care facilities all over the world.

Telemedicine is still relatively new and is changing rapidly. It has benefited from advances in telecommunications, efficiencies, and lowered costs of technology and widespread use of the Internet. Start-up costs are no longer prohibitive for most practitioners. Indeed, the real costs today are not in purchasing and setting up the equipment but in integrating telemedicine into existing health systems. Of course, with the advances in the development and use of telemedicine also come numerous legal questions including physician licensing and malpractice liability.

B.   LICENSING AND ACCREDITATION

Each state regulates the practice of medicine within its borders. All state licensing statutes require physicians to be licensed in the state before they can practice medicine in that state. When a physician delivers medical services via telemedicine to a patient located in the same state in which he is licensed to practice medicine, there is no licensing issue because the physician is practicing within the scope of his license.

Licensing problems arise when a physician seeks to deliver medical services via telemedicine to a patient located in an area outside of that in which he is licensed to practice medicine. In that case the physician seeks to practice medicine across the state line and would need to obtain a license to practice medicine in the state where the patient is located. The law holds that the "practice" of medicine occurs in the location that treatment occurs. Of course, requiring physicians to become licensed to practice medicine in every state where the telecommunications would extend would render telemedicine extremely burdensome and increase its costs. Consequently, solutions to both the out-of-state and multi-state licensure problems are being evaluated. A variety of licensure options are being explored and debated. Some of these options include: allowing an out-of-state practitioner to act as a consultant in a different state; establishing licensing reciprocity between states; creating licensing on a limited basis within a state; and eliminating state licensing in favor of licensure at the national level.

Many states already have already adopted some form of licensure provision to address the use of telemedicine within their borders. For example, Texas has adopted a "special purpose license" system that allows physicians outside of Texas to practice medicine within the state. Although Texas law requires that a medical examination of any patient in the state to be performed by a practitioner licensed by the state, the law contains exceptions for "episodic and informal consultations," emergencies, and medical school consultations. As of the year 2000, twenty states had enacted statutes similar to that of Texas. Furthermore, three states permitted telemedicine "reciprocity" such that physicians could practice within the state to the extent that their own state laws recognize the practice. Twenty-eight states had taken no action as to licensure for telemedicine consultations as of the year 2002.

In addition to state licensing law, private accrediting bodies such as the Joint Commission on Accreditation of Healthcare Organizations (JCAHO) require covered facilities to "credential" medical staff members to ensure their competence. JCAHO has established guidelines for the accreditation of healthcare networks, but as yet it has not yet addressed many of the legal issues specific to telemedicine. Such issues as whether physicians must be admitted to the host facility's medical staff to admit patients and whether physicians must be proficient in telemedicine practice have yet to be addressed.

C. PRIVACY ISSUES

The practice of telemedicine requires that patient information be electronically transmitted across state lines. Demands for patient privacy require that medical records have a custodian who is responsible making patient information available to authorized users and maintaining its confidentiality in all other circumstances. For the most part, state and local laws govern data protection for the privacy and confidentiality of patient information. State guidelines vary even as to such basic issues as the acceptability of an electronic signature. Telemedicine creates new opportunities for violations of patient privacy that leaves facilities and practitioners vulnerable to disclosure of inaccurate or confidential medical information.

The Health Insurance Portability and Accountability Act (HIPAA), signed into law in 1996 and implemented in 2003 addresses some of the concerns common to telemedicine. HIPAA's Privacy Rule covers most health care plans and providers who utilize electronic transmission of patient health information. It creates national standards for the protection of individuals' medical records, and is intended to improve the efficiency and effectiveness of the healthcare system by encouraging the development of health information systems that comply with HIPAA guidelines. Covered entities practicing telemedicine have the benefit of HIPAA compliance guidelines to address these privacy issues.

D. MALPRACTICE LIABILITY

The four major elements of a malpractice negligence action in conventional medicine, duty, breach, causation, and damages, are also the essential elements of a telemedicine malpractice claim. In light of the special considerations applicable to telemedicine, a body of law is not yet developed to determine whether, and under what circumstances, the essential elements of the malpractice action have been met. For example, the nature of the physician–patient relationship and the scope of the duty of the telemedicine consultant is likely to give rise to a new body of legal principles.

When and where a telemedicine consult would give rise to a physician-patient relationship is unclear. Generally a physician-patient relationship arises when a physician delivers medical services to a patient that contracted for these services. Through the use of telemedicine, a physician-patient relationship could arise between parties that are hundreds of miles apart. Courts have addressed this issue generally, when considering whether physician consultations over the telephone have resulted in a physician-patient relationship. While no case involving telemedicine has yet been litigated, related legal principles may be instructive. For example, a Texas Court of Appeals maintained that a mere phone call was not enough to establish a doctor-patient relationship when there was not some other affirmative action on the part of the physician to create such a relationship. In *Majzoub v. Appling* (Tex.App.2002), the court concluded that recommendations made by the defendant on-call physician to the treating physician, which did not include providing a diagnosis or making medical decisions, did not rise to the level of a physician-patient relationship. In contrast, another Texas Court of Appeals reversed a summary judgment in favor of an on-call physician who made a diagnosis and developed a treatment plan over the telephone, which the treating physician relied upon. In *Lection v. Dyll* (Tex.App.2001). The court was unable to conclude whether a physician-patient relationship existed, and remanded the case for further proceedings.

Negligence theory requires health care systems to credential and supervise staff as well as independent physicians providing care under the auspices of the system. It is unclear whether a telemedicine host, with no other affiliation to a remote physician or hospital other than the network, might still be liable for the negligence of a remote treating physician. Does the network incur a duty to supervise all of its remote partners in their use of the telemedicine system? Might the host be held to exercise control over network activities?

Finally, if a physician-patient relationship is established, there still exists a question as to which state laws apply to a potential malpractice action. Rules have yet to be established as to which jurisdictional laws apply when a consultation involves physicians and patients located in different states. As to the applicable standard of patient care, most jurisdictions are moving away from regional or locality considerations toward a nationalized professional standard. The telemedicine consultant, who is likely to be selected on the basis of expertise, should expect to be held to a high standard of patient care.

CHAPTER TWELVE

LIABILITY OF MANAGED CARE ORGANIZATIONS

A. DEVELOPMENT OF MANAGED CARE ORGANIZATIONS

Managed care organizations (MCOs) arose in response to escalating costs of medical services in the 1970s and 1980s. Before development of the MCO, medical services in the United States were traditionally paid on a "fee-for-service" basis. In a fee-for-service system, insurance companies would allow the patient to select a health care provider and provide coverage for any desired service or procedures that the physician determined was necessary. The insurance company would then pay the physician for services rendered. The physician had incentive to order many tests and provide many services because his compensation increased with each service that he ordered. In addition, physicians often felt pressure to practice so-called "defensive" medicine—ordering numerous medical services to rule out any possible condition. This approach included many potentially unnecessary tests in order to avoid a future malpractice lawsuit by their patients. Ever increasing fee-for-service spending is thought to have contributed to exorbitant health care costs and ever-increasing annual costs for health care services, and health care insurers were among those that sought a different method for the delivery and payment of health care services.

MCOs are systems that contractually integrate health care delivery and financing, and attempt to manage both the cost of service and quality of care that the MCO provides to the patients enrolled in the plan. The more popular forms of MCOs include health maintenance organizations (HMOs), independent practice associations (IPAs), and preferred-provider organizations (PPOs). As of 2001, more than seventy percent of employees in the United States were enrolled in some type of MCO.

MCOs attempt to reduce the costs associated with health care through many different mechanisms. Some establish preferred provider networks that limit the patient's choice of health care provider. Physicians enrolled with the MCO receive care from what is commonly referred to as network physician. The network physicians are contractually bound to provide only authorized services to plan participants, and will not be reimbursed by the MCO for costs or services above that agreed upon amount. Additionally, MCOs may attempt to limit the types of treatments that a patient may receive. MCOs reduce costs by requiring pre-certification, or pre-utilization review for certain procedures to determine whether they are medically necessary. MCOs also may develop incentives for physicians to provide less care through capitation plans or risk-sharing arrangements. Under a capitation plan, the

MCO will pay a provider a contractually agreed upon annual amount for each plan participant, without consideration for the type or amount of services administered during a specific time period. Under a risk-sharing arrangement, the MCO will withhold a portion of each physician's capitation payment and pool it with the capitation payments of other physicians in order to pay for expenses including referrals, unanticipated hospital stays or expensive procedures. These incentives make it more financially advantageous for the health care provider to administer fewer services to the beneficiaries of the plan.

B.   MCO LIABILITY

The contractual arrangement between physicians and MCOs generally provides that the MCO is not responsible for any negligence of the physician, and the physician must hold the MCO harmless in case of a lawsuit alleging medical negligence. Nevertheless, there are several state law theories under which legal action has been brought against MCOs by patients who are harmed by a physician engaged by an MCO. These include vicarious liability, ostensible agency, negligent credentialing, negligent utilization review, and negligence per se. While each of these theories may be the basis of a viable claim against a MCO, there is a federal law known as the Employee Retirement Income Security Act of 1974 (ERISA), 29 U.S.C. § 1001 *et seq.* which, if applicable, preempts state law as to the regulation of employee benefit plans. ERISA preempts state law to the extent that the patient obtains his medical insurance as part of an employee benefit plan and state law purports to impose substantive provisions (i.e. negligence) other than those pertaining to the relation of insurance. Whether ERISA preempts a state liability claim is a complex factual issue that has been the subject of recent Supreme Court scrutiny. ERISA preemption will be discussed *infra*.

1. Vicarious Liability

Under the theory of vicarious liability, MCOs may be held liable for the conduct of a physician that is affiliated with the MCO. The doctrine is based on the agency theory of liability in which an employer is held responsible for the negligent acts of its employees. Vicarious liability is most applicable when HMOs employ physicians directly, but can also be successfully asserted against HMOs that contract with independent physicians under the control of the HMO. In *Schleier v. Kaiser Found. Health Plan* (D.C.Cir.1989), the federal district court considered the following five factors in order to determine if a "master-servant" or agency relationship existed for the purposes of finding an HMO liable for an independent contractor physician's negligence: "(1) the selection and engagement of the servant, (2) the payment of wages, (3) the power to discharge, (4) the power to control the servant's conduct, (5) and whether the work is part of the regular business of the employer." The court upheld the finding of vicarious liability for the HMO on the basis that there was enough evidence to support a finding that the HMO had control over the physician, even though he was an independent contractor.

2. Apparent or Ostensible Agency

In many circumstances the court may find that the physician is not an agent of the MCO, and a claim against the MCO for vicarious liability for the actions of the treating physician will not be sustained. In instances where an MCO engages in conduct that could reasonably lead a patient to believe that the physician was acting as the agent of the MCO, for example, a claim for apparent or ostensible agency may be appropriate, and the MCO may be held liable for the negligence of the treating physician. In deciding whether to apply the doctrine of apparent agency, courts generally will consider: "(1) whether the patient looks to the institution, rather than the individual physician for care, and (2) whether the HMO 'holds out' the physician as its employee." *Boyd v. Albert Einstein Med. Ctr.* (Pa.Super.1988).

In *Boyd*, the court considered whether actions taken by the defendant HMO could have led to the decedent's reasonable belief that her physician was an agent of the HMO. The court considered the contract between the decedent and the HMO in which the HMO agreed to provide health care services to promote the health of the patient on a direct service basis. Additionally, the court considered the HMO's provider list of primary physicians and the screening requirements the physicians needed to comply with. In reversing the trial court's grant of summary judgment for the HMO, the court held that there was an issue of material fact as to whether the HMO had conducted itself in a manner that would make it reasonable for the decedent to believe the physician was an agent of the HMO.

3. Negligent Credentialing

The development of preferred provider lists by many MCOs has raised the issue of whether the MCO may be held liable for failing to adequately screen the credentials of the physicians that it includes on its panels. Under this theory of liability, the plaintiff must demonstrate both that the MCO was negligent in investigating the background and skill level of the physician, and that the physician was negligent in treating the patient. Claims relating to negligent credentialing may also be implicated when considering ERISA preemption and are discussed *infra*.

4. Negligent Utilization Review

MCOs use various forms of utilization review as methods for reducing the exorbitant costs associated with health care. MCOs may require a physician to get prior approval before treating a patient with a particular drug, referring the patient to a specialist, performing a certain procedure, or extending the length of a hospital stay. Although this reduces costs, it can also be a basis for litigation if a patient is not satisfied with the care he or she received. There is much debate as to whether the MCO's failure to approve a certain treatment is a decision about administration of benefits, or a decision related to quality of medical care. This is central to the inquiry of whether a claim may be preempted by ERISA.

5. Negligence Per Se

An MCO may face liability when physicians or other health care providers working under its direction violate a statute. Pursuant to the doctrine of negligence *per se*, violation of a statute may constitute negligence *per se* if the plaintiff can establish the following: (1) the injured person is a member of the class of individuals that the statute was enacted to protect; (2) the alleged harm was the type of harm that the statute was enacted to protect against; and (3) there is a causal connection between the violation of the statute and the damage suffered by the plaintiff. *Rockefeller v. Kaiser Found. Health Plan of Georgia* (Ga.App.2001). The *Rockefeller* court upheld summary judgment against an HMO when health care providers working with the HMO violated a statute that required physician's assistants to be supervised by board-approved physicians before administering treatment or prescriptions to patients. At issue was a preliminary diagnosis and treatment decision made by a physician's assistant that was approved by a non-board-approved physician. The plaintiff maintained that the health care providers were negligent in misdiagnosing her pneumonia and she sustained permanent disabilities resulting from improper treatment.

The court concluded that the statute restricting physician's assistants to work under board-approved physicians supervision only was designed to protect patients from the type of harm that the plaintiff alleged. It held that this violation constituted negligence *per se.*

C. THE EMPLOYEE RETIREMENT INCOME SECURITY ACT OF 1974

1. ERISA Generally

In 1974 Congress enacted ERISA as a means of encouraging national employers to provide employee benefits by allowing them uniform regulation under this federal scheme rather than subjecting them to state-by-state laws. ERISA regulates the administration of benefit plans, participation and vesting requirements and the fiduciary responsibilities of plan administrators. In these areas where it is applicable, it preempts state law that conflicts with its provisions. ERISA has a broad reach in that it covers any plan that satisfies the following elements:

"(1) A 'plan, fund, or program' (2) established or maintained (3) by an employer or by employee organization, or by both, (4) for the purpose of providing medical, surgical, hospital care, sickness, accident, disability, death, unemployment or vacation benefits, apprenticeship or other training programs, day care centers, scholarship funds, prepaid legal services or severance benefits (5) to the participants or their beneficiaries."

McClellan v. Health Maint. Org. of Pa. (Pa.Super.1992). Although ERISA mandates that state laws relating to employee benefit plans are preempted, it contains two provisions that may affect preemption. First, a "savings clause" allows that state laws pertaining to the "regulation" of insurance, banking, securities, and generally applicable criminal laws are not preempted. 29 U.S.C. § 1144(b)(2)(a) (2002). Secondly, the ERISA "deemer" clause provides that states may not "deem" an employee benefit plan an insurance company in order to qualify for the insurance law exception (and thus avoid preemption). 29 U.S.C. § 1144(b)(2)(b).

Whether a claim is preempted by ERISA will have a significant effect on the potential liability of an MCO. Under ERISA, plan participants may only seek to (1) recover benefits owed to them pursuant to the terms of the contract, (2) enforce benefits due to them under the contract, (3) clarify rights to future benefits under the contract, or (4) establish other "equitable relief." 29 U.S.C. § 1132(a)(1), (3) (2002). In five separate cases, the circuits courts in the United States Court of Appeals have interpreted this limitation on available remedies to preclude beneficiaries under an ERISA plan from receiving either punitive or compensatory damages. Thus whether a claim falls within the reach of ERISA is of great interest to both MCOs and plan participants.

2. Preemption of State Law Claims Under ERISA

According to section 514(a) of the statute, ERISA will preempt any state law if it "relates to" an employee benefit plan. 29 U.S.C. § 1144(a) (2002). In interpreting whether a claim relates to a benefit plan, courts may attempt to distinguish between claims that involve "quality of care" and those that involve provision of benefits. Generally, allegations that the MCO provided poor quality of care will not be preempted by ERISA, and the plaintiffs will be allowed state law remedies. If a claim relates to the provision of benefits under a contract, however, ERISA will likely preempt the claim, and the plan beneficiary's remedies will be limited to those provided under the contract.

Courts have held that state law claims against a MCO are not preempted by ERISA when the alleged wrongdoing involves a medical treatment decision, or quality of care decision, made by the MCO. For example, the Third Circuit Court of Appeals concluded that negligence and vicarious liability claims against an HMO were not preempted by ERISA when a hospital, working through the HMO, refused to perform blood tests that the decedent's physician ordered. *Dukes v. U.S. Healthcare, Inc.* (3d Cir.1995). The court, noting that this was a quality of care issue, explained that the plaintiff's allegations focused on the poor quality of medical treatment and were not concerned with provision of benefits, i.e., whether the HMO would pay for the blood test. The court also commented that Congress' silence on quality of care within the ERISA statute should be interpreted as leaving that issue to traditional state regulation.

Similarly, the Third Circuit Court of Appeals determined that when an HMO is providing medical treatment, through its practices and policies, the HMO is still subject to state laws regarding standard of care. *In re U.S. Healthcare, Inc.* (3d Cir. 1999). The court addressed several claims against an HMO related to its policy for discharging mothers and new babies from the hospital within twenty-four hours after the baby's birth. In *U.S. Healthcare*, a baby became ill within two days of release from the hospital. Despite repeated efforts by the baby's parents to get help from the treating physician and the HMO, the baby's strep infection was not detected or treated, and the baby died. The court considered whether direct negligence and vicarious liability claims against the HMO were preempted by ERISA. In concluding they were not preempted, the court held that the HMO was acting as a medical services provider when it allegedly adopted policies that encouraged physicians to release infants within twenty-four hours of their birth, and discouraged physicians from re-admitting those infants into the hospital. The court held that the claims were not related to the provision of benefits under the beneficiary's contract and therefore were not preempted under ERISA.

Claims involving administration of benefits according to the contract between the MCO and the plan beneficiary fall squarely into provision of benefits claims that are preempted by ERISA. In *Pryzbowski v. U.S. Healthcare* (3d Cir.2001), a plaintiff claimed that her HMO negligently and arbitrarily delayed approval of surgery on her back, allegedly leading to severe and persistent back pain. The court concluded that this claim related to a HMO's approval of benefits and that it was preempted by ERISA. The court held that any other holding "would open the door for legal challenges to core managed care practices."

Preemption determinations are more difficult, however, when the claim are neither pure "coverage" or "quality of care" decisions but are "mixed" determinations concerning medical necessity or utilization. In *Calad v. Cigna Healthcare of Tex.* (N.D.Tex.2001), a Texas District Court concluded that the plaintiff's claim that her HMO negligently adhered to its medical necessity criteria was preempted by ERISA. In *Calad*, the plaintiff alleged that her HMO negligently adhered to its plan protocols when it pre-authorized only one day of hospitalization subsequent to a vaginal hysterectomy, releasing her from the hospital the following day because she did not meet its criteria of medical necessity. This would have included symptoms of hemorrhaging, fever, or high blood pressure. The court held that allegations regarding both the pre-surgery authorization of the hospital stay and the post-surgery release from the hospital both ultimately concerned the amount and types of services that the plaintiff was entitled to according to her HMO plan. The court classified these determinations as related to quantity of care, and concluded that they were preempted by ERISA.

3. The Fiduciary Duty Owed Under ERISA

In order to be considered a fiduciary under the terms of ERISA, a person must serve as a manager, administrator, or financial advisor to an ERISA plan. *See* 29 U.S.C. §§ 1002 (21)(A)(i)-(iii) (2002); *Pegram v. Herdrich* (S.Ct.2000). The fiduciary is held to the "prudent man" standard of care and must act "for the exclusive purpose of (i) providing benefits to participants and their beneficiaries; and (ii) defraying reasonable expenses of administering the plan." 29 U.S.C. § 1104(a)(1)(A), (B) (2002). As plan administrators, advisors, and managers will also have non-fiduciary roles as they carry out their duties, ERISA only requires that they act as fiduciaries to the extent that they are acting in a that capacity regarding the plan. Whether an act is considered "fiduciary" under ERISA has been the subject of much litigation.

The question of whether plan administrators are acting in a fiduciary capacity is particularly troublesome when a claim involves financial incentives used by an HMO to reduce costs. The Supreme Court of the United States determined that the HMO was not acting in a fiduciary capacity when its physician made a "mixed treatment and eligibility" decision. In *Pegram v. Herdrich* (S.Ct.2000) a plaintiff alleged that an HMO breached its fiduciary duty under ERISA by allowing the HMO's financial incentives to encourage the treating physician to act in a manner contrary to her best interests. Although the treating physician diagnosed an inflamed mass in the patient's abdomen, she did not believe it to be an emergent condition. The physician recommended that the patient did not need an immediate ultrasound at a non-HMO affiliated local hospital, but instead could wait more than a week to have the procedure performed at a distant facility owned by the HMO. Before the patient received an ultrasound, her appendix ruptured and she became ill. The Court reasoned that in this case, the eligibility decision could not be separated from the medical treatment decision: if the physician determined the patient's condition was emergent, the HMO would have paid for an immediate ultrasound. In ruling in favor of the HMO, the Court concluded that Congress did not intend for ERISA's fiduciary duty to be extended to cover these mixed treatment and eligibility decisions.

A recent divided opinion by the second circuit in *Cicio v. Vytra* Healthcare (2d Cir.2003) demonstrates the uncertainty and discomfort with the Supreme Court's decision in *Pegram*. Once again, a mixed treatment and eligibility decision was at issue when a patient's HMO denied coverage for a tandem stem cell transplant for a patient diagnosed with multiple myeloma. The HMO characterized the procedure as experimental and denied it on that basis. The lower court dismissed the action on the basis of ERISA preemption, and *Pegram*, finding that it was a mixed treatment and eligibility matter governed by *Pegram*.

The second circuit disagreed, but a vigorous dissent by Judge Calabresi makes it clear that the issue is still unsettled. The two-judge majority distinguished Pegram, holding that while it was the physician in *Pegram* that made the treatment decision (perhaps with financial motives in mind), in *Cicio* it was the HMO that made the "treatment" decision by refusing coverage for the transplant and even suggesting an alternative procedure. Thus the court held that the HMO could be accountable for its own medical malpractice. Note that that matter was not brought under the doctrine of respondeat superior as the physician was not employed by the HMO and further, he recommended the procedure. ERISA would not preempt malpractice actions on that basis. Although not a novel theory, this was the first time post-Pegram that an appellate court held that an HMO directly was making a treatment decision in its decision to deny treatment.

In general, courts have interpreted ERISA so as to not impose a fiduciary duty on an HMO to automatically disclose all of its financial incentives or physician compensation schemes to plan participants. In *Peterson v. Connecticut Gen. Life Ins. Co.* (E.D.Pa.2000), a federal District Court refused to uphold a claim for breach of fiduciary duty when an HMO failed to disclose all of its financial incentives, compensation arrangements and treatment guidelines to a plan participant. The court held that the legislature was better suited to create such a broad fiduciary duty and noted that the plaintiff could access much of the information she requested on the defendant's website.

In *Ehlmann v. Kaiser Found. Health Plan of Tex.* (5th Cir.2000) the Fifth Circuit reached a similar result when it concluded that ERISA imposes no duty on an HMO to disclose its physician compensation scheme. The court noted that ERISA does have detailed disclosure obligations, but that none of them include physician compensation, and that creating such requirements is most suited for the legislature. *See* 29 U.S.C. §§ 1021–1031 (2002).

Courts have interpreted ERISA to impose a fiduciary duty on HMOs to disclose financial incentives in some instances where the incentive may discourage specialized care that the patient needs. In *Shea v. Esensten* (8th Cir.1997) the Eighth Circuit reviewed a breach of fiduciary duty claim after a primary care physician discouraged a man from seeing a cardiologist, even though he was complaining of chest pains, dizziness, shortness of breath, and had an extensive family history of heart disease. Under the terms of the patient's contract with his HMO, he needed a physician's referral before he could access a specialist. The patient was unaware that the HMO discouraged referrals by creating financial incentives for physicians to make fewer referrals by withholding the pay of physicians who made too many referrals. The patient never was referred to a cardiologist and died a few months later. The court held that the decedent should have been informed of the HMO's incentive plan that discouraged its physicians from making referrals so he could have made an informed decision about whether his physician's judgment might have been clouded by such incentives. The case was remanded for further proceedings.

Courts have also interpreted the fiduciary duty under ERISA to include the duty to convey accurate information that is material to a beneficiary's circumstance. This includes a duty to "inform when the trustee knows that silence might be harmful" as well as a duty not to misinform. *Bixler v. Central Pa. Teamsters Health and Welfare Fund* (3d Cir. 1993). In *Bixler*, plaintiff alleged that her decedent husband's employer was liable for breach of ERISA's fiduciary duty when it failed to notify her that she might be eligible for unpaid medical expenses. She had called to inquire about whether she was eligible for death benefits. The court remanded the case for determination of the circumstances of plaintiff's inquiry and whether the employer was acting in a fiduciary capacity, whether the employer was aware of the plaintiff's special circumstances, and finally whether the employer violated the fiduciary duty under ERISA.

D. CONCLUSION

The question of who should held accountable for an inappropriate medical decision is of great interest to MCOs, health care providers, and patients. Given the complexity of the managed care system, in that it combines health care treatment decisions with health care administration and financing, it is unlikely that this question will be answered without legislative involvement. Although MCOs may be held accountable for state law actions that are related to medical treatment, or quality of care decisions, ERISA preempts state law claims concerning administration decisions, or quantity of care decisions, made by the MCO. It is likely that this area of law will evolve as MCOs, federal, and state laws continue to develop.

*

INDEX

References are to Pages

311

†